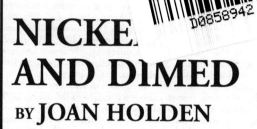

NICKEL
AND DIMED
BY JOAN HOLDEN

**Based on *Nickel and Dimed*,
on (Not) Getting by in America
by Barbara Ehrenreich**

★

★

DRAMATISTS
PLAY SERVICE
INC.

NICKEL AND DIMED
Copyright © 2005, Joan Holden

All Rights Reserved

THE BOOK AND THE PLAY

Barbara Ehrenreich's first-person account of her journey through low-wage jobs was a national bestseller, 2001–2004. To make a play from this nonfiction book, I condensed some characters and scenes, expanded others, left out some, and invented some based on slight suggestions, or on conversations with the real Barbara. I have kept a lot of the original language: Barbara's funniest lines come straight from the book.

FURTHER ACKNOWLEDGMENTS

Bart Sher heard Barbara on the radio and imagined the play; he commissioned me to write it. Gordon Davidson and Oskar Eustis gave it second and third lives; Mame Hunt, Oskar Eustis, Craig Lucas, Daniel Chumley, and Kevin Moriarty proposed major improvements.

Mame Hunt unearthed employment questionnaires; Kate Godman taught me a chambermaid's routine. Angry audience members at talk-backs in Seattle and Los Angeles provided the Boyfriend's arguments.

The play was developed backward: The first draft was splendidly produced, then the script got revised. The heavy work, after the Intiman, was done at the Mark Taper Forum, where the original production reopened after rewrites; the Trinity Repertory Company (who also made it possible for me to spend time with Barbara); and the Guthrie Lab, where Bill Rauch directed and Robynn Rodgriguez played Barbara. More revisions were made at Heritage Theatre Company; Naked Eye; Curious Theatre Company; TheaterWorks; Brava! for Women in the Arts; and the Philadelphia Theatre Company. All the revisions, early and late, were made thanks to the generosity and gameness of more actors, directors and dramaturgs than I can name.

Thank you to Barbara, for having the guts to take the journey and the wit to write about it, and to all the above.

—*Joan Holden*

NOTES FOR PRODUCTION

STYLE AND PACE: Epic/comic, not naturalistic, although the psychology is real. Don't play for laughs except in the farce scenes, but keep up a comic pace without pauses except in the few intimate scenes, and keep transitions fluid. In the restaurant scenes, the place is crowded and everyone is forced to work at top speed, except after their shift, in the locker room.

MUSIC: The script assumes transition music and sometimes underscoring. The play wants to get under people's skin, and it's about work, so music should be live, not recorded, and the working musician(s) should be visible, in the house.

SCENE SIGNS: At each place Barbara works and at each place she stays, the wages paid or rent charged should be displayed: These are given in scene headings in the script.

"BREAKOUT" SCENE: This works well where many in the audience have cleaning help and the actors can also afford it, when it is played with maximum heat and self-righteousness. We lower the audience's defenses against our message by making fools of ourselves. If the scene is wrong for the audience or unbelievable to the cast, cut it: Go from "the American upper middle class sheds at a truly alarming rate" to "agh: The chemicals I'm saving Holly from… "

MALL-MART: Scene sign should not go up until Barbara says the name. The store floor should not be revealed till Barbara's first day on the job — ideally on "Mall-mart family values."

INTERMISSION: after ACT TWO.

NOTES ON CHARACTERS

BARBARA: She is a scientist. Her main action is to discover the truth and share it. Thus she often throws the focus to other characters and lets them take over the stage. Her personal story is not the main subject of the book or the play. Barbara's near-constant irony isn't angry: It's how she sublimates anger. Played angry, she will weary the audience. She sometimes indulges in altruistic rage, as in the speech aimed at the rich lady — but doesn't get personally, selfishly angry till the mad scene in Mall-mart. Once she has backed into this assignment, she embraces it. In Florida, she learns the rules of the game; in Maine, she tries to help; in Minnesota, after two failures, she's tired out and just struggles to survive.

GAIL: A great waitress, never out of work. She moves at breakneck speed and has always outrun her problems, but they're starting to catch up.

JOAN: Captain of the ship. Part of her job is to raise the energy level. Her sex jokes and flirting are performance: She doesn't fraternize and the men know it.

CARLIE: Long ago, she was full of rage; it burned down to disgust. Now she wastes no calories either on being mad at people or on trying to please them.

PETE: He's not bragging, or Barbara couldn't have a soft spot for him; he's sharing his dreams.

HOLLY: Her recent promotion to Team Leader makes her the biggest success in her family. She is terrified she will fail Ted and make him demote her.

MADDY: Challenges authority as a matter of self-respect. When she talks to her little son locked in the motel room, she cannot let him hear her panic.

MARGE: The only woman we meet who has a happy home life.

MELISSA: The audience laughs at her zeal at first; they stop laughing when they see she is truly a good Christian.

5

THE BOYFRIEND: He dismisses Barbara's project at first (his brief appearance in the first flashback); when she heads out again (the bus station) he gets mad — not just because she leaves home, but because her very premise — that all people deserve decent and decently paid work — challenges his pride in what he has individually achieved. When she crashes in Maine, he thinks she's beaten, so can afford, briefly, to be magnanimous.

PHILIP: Desperate to succeed, and constantly being sabotaged.

GEORGE: Knows he's cute and uses that.

THE SOCIAL WORKER: Wants to help but almost never can.

VERY IMPORTANT: None of Barbara' fellow-workers complains. These people do not see themselves as victims; they all play the hands they were dealt.

NICKEL AND DIMED was originally produced at the Intiman Theatre (Bartlett Sher, Artistic Director; Laura Penn, Managing Director) in Seattle, Washington, opening on August 2, 2002. It was directed by Bartlett Sher; the set design was by John Arnone; the costume design was by Rose Pederson; the lighting design was by Mary Louise Geiger; the original music and sound design were by Michael McQuilken; the stage manager was J.R. Welden; and the dramaturg was Mame Hunt. The cast was as follows:

GAIL	Christine McMurdo-Wallis
BARBARA	Sharon Lockwood
NITA	Cynthia Jones
GEORGE	Jason Cottle
HECTOR	Olga Sanchez
JOAN	Kristin Flanders

CHARACTERS

Doubling as indicated:

GAIL, waitress, late 40s–50s
Actor also plays:
> Winn-Dixie manager (a man)
> Marge, maid, 60s
> Rich Lady

BARBARA, 50s

CARLIE, hotel maid, 50s
Actor also plays:
> Nita, waitress, 30s
> Phillip, Kenny's manager, West Indian, 30s
> Nanny in Maine, any age
> Melissa, Mall-mart associate, late 40s–early 50s

GEORGE, busboy, 20s
Actor also plays:
> Editor, 60s
> Boyfriend, successful writer, 50s
> Pete, nursing home cook, 40s
> Ted, Magic Maids' franchise owner, 30s
> Howard, Mall-mart assistant manager, 20s

HECTOR, 30s
Actor also plays:
> Maddy, maid, 20s
> Kimberly, Mall-mart associate, 20s

JOAN, Kenny's hostess, 40
Actor also plays:
> Holly, maid, early 20s

ENSEMBLE

Restaurant customers; servers in Manhattan; nursing home patients; Mall-mart customers.

The play is written for a cast of six: five women — three white, one African-American, one Latina and Spanish-speaking — and one white man.

PLACE and TIME

America, 1990s.

NICKEL AND DIMED

ACT ONE — FLORIDA

Scene 1

Kenny's, $2.15 per hour, plus tips. Barbara, Gail, Nita, George, Hector.

Gail enters carrying a laden tray. At warp speed, she waits on invisible customers as Barbara trots behind her pouring coffee and water. Gail is onstage — bright and cheerful — with the customers; offstage — matter-of-fact — with Barbara, who has passed herself off as experienced. Gail feels a migraine coming on, and did not expect to be training someone today. Throughout the following, kitchen bell periodically goes "bing" upstage; Nita, with condiment caddy and order book, and George with bus tray crisscross among tables, ordering computer, and kitchen. Barbara tries in vain to keep up and prove she knows the ropes, but she gets more and more lost.

GAIL. Okay, here's how the tables go: Booths are three to eighteen, counting by threes, little tables are even numbers up to twenty, middle aisle just count by tens. You got that, right?
BARBARA. Um —
GAIL. *(To customers.)* Okay, we had a Li'l Abner, a Snuffy Smith ... Barbara'll get your coffee — *(Barbara hurries to pour and nearly trips. To customers.)* — A Swee'pea and a Daisy Mae. *(Gail sees a customer signaling at another table, calls.)* Hi, Mr. Goldman! My personal assistant — she'll get your coffee.
BARBARA. Right up! *(Barbara hurries to pour.)*
GAIL. *(Picking up an earlier conversation at another table.)* Where

from in Illinois? ... How far's that from Kankakee? That's where my dad lives ... Oh, then you wouldn't know 'im. Heck, I don't either. Here we go, Blueberry, Honey, and Maple ... Extra butter — don't let my manager see this, but *I* know two pats of butter'll get lost in those hotcakes. Just yell if you need anything, okay? *(To Barbara.)* I don't care about the rest of your side work, but keep your sugars filled and what Tina Turner over there — *(Indicates Nita.)* — never does, always wipe your syrup bottoms or else you get flies.

BARBARA. Okay.

GAIL. They had *her* train you, you'd be marrying your ketchups in front of your customers. *(George enters with tray, clears a table, nods to women.)*

GAIL. Hey Georgie — don't let me catch you flirting with her: You're *my* sweetie! *(George smiles, exits.)* You can say anything: He don't understand English. From Poland or Yugoslavia or someplace. Okay. You know how to use a computer?

BARBARA. Yes.

GAIL. Okay, table number ... *(Demonstrates.)* server number — did they give you one?

BARBARA. No ... *(She tries to fathom unfamiliar touch-screen.)*

GAIL. For today, ninety-nine ... *(Touch-orders rapidly as she talks.)* They give you trouble, it was my idea — number of people at the table. Modify over here. Leave your finger there too long, you've ordered fifty-five sets of hash-browns. Other thing you gotta remember with this one: After you order, hit Clear before you hit Send. You got that, right?

BARBARA. That makes no sense!

GAIL. Trust me. And hey. You know when Philip said if you have a problem, take it to him?

BARBARA. Right —

GAIL. Don't take it to him. He'll mess you *all* up, telling you what to do and he's never done it. It was a twerp like him made me swear I'd never work for another chain. You give and you give, and they take and they take. And *now* look at me. I only took this job 'cause my boyfriend got killed.

BARBARA. Oh, my God!

GAIL. In a knife fight, in prison upstate. He was only in there for DUI. I couldn't sleep right for three months. Then I let his best friend move in to help with the rent, and he's the reason I got this headache. Okay, soon's you order, get their juice: Give 'em something to suck on. *(Three customers — couple with teenager — enter and sit.)* Fifteen's yours! *(Projection appears: $2.15/hr + tips.)* Menus. Don't forget to ask Link or Patty. Don't worry, you'll be fine: You're surrounded by my golden circle of light. *(She exits.)*

BARBARA. Good morning and welcome to Kenny's! *(Passing out menus.)* Where you folks from?

MAN. Montana.

BARBARA. Fantastic! I was born in Butte! *(They don't answer.)* Would you like coffee while you look at the menu?

MAN. We don't drink coffee.

WOMAN. We don't need the menu: We know what we want.

TEENAGER. I don't want anything. *(Barbara, trying a joke, writes.)* "Nothing."

WOMAN. She'll have oatmeal and tomato juice.

TEENAGER. … Diet Coke and an English muffin.

MAN. Gimme a Snuffy with tomato juice, eggs sunny-side up, sausage, wheat toast.

BARBARA. Link or patty? *(Man stares at her.)* Would that be sausage patties, or link sausages?

MAN. How many?

BARBARA. … I'm new. I could ask …

MAN. *(Long-suffering.)* Christ. Just bring me the patty.

WOMAN. A Daisy Mae with tomato juice, and could I have canned prunes instead of potatoes?

BARBARA. I'll see if that's okay.

WOMAN. It is. Two eggs poached, very, very runny and wheat toast, very, very light.

BARBARA. *(Checking the menu.)* I don't think we have poached eggs …

WOMAN. I always have them. I'm sure your cook can poach an egg.

BARBARA. … I'll ask him. *(To teenager.)* So … English muffin?

WOMAN. She'll have oatmeal.

BARBARA. … Oatmeal.

WOMAN. Our Kenny's gives me prunes.

BARBARA. Coming right up. *(She heads for computer. Doesn't know how to boot up order screen, makes two false tries, gets it. Meanwhile, the family argues sotto voce. Nita arrives in line.)* Table … Fifteen … Server … Ninety-nine … Customers … three … Snuffy … sausage … patty … Daisy Mae …

NITA. The way it works, the train's supposed to move, not the station.

13

BARBARA. I'm sorry ... I'm trying to modify potatoes to prunes?

NITA. Like this. *(She enters the order.)* Who had the bright idea to make you work breakfast? Let's take a *wild* guess — Philip.

BARBARA. Thanks. Now I have to ask for poached eggs?

NITA. ... Hit Verbal. *(Barbara touches screen. Disaster.)* That was Void!!! I have a table of eight.

BARBARA. Why don't you just go ahead? *(Nita does.)*

GAIL. *(Arrives in line.)* You never want to rush Mr. Goldman! Five bucks. *(Displays her tip.)* Hey Nita: How 'bout I order my three tables, then can you finish whatever it is you're doing?

NITA. How 'bout you kiss my sticky buns? *(Nita exits.)*

BARBARA. It's my fault. I held her up. Tell me if I've got this. For poached eggs —

GAIL. Oh, Jesus.

BARBARA. I hit Verbal ...

GAIL. ... then run fast as you can and tell Hector. Then, duck. He's drinkin' today.

BARBARA. Hector? The one that was throwing steaks at the wall when I came in?

GAIL. The night cook forgot to defrost 'em. Gimme your ticket and go talk to Hector. *(Barbara exits with expression of gratitude. Man gets up, crosses to Gail.)*

MAN. How long does it take to make eggs?

GAIL. *(Without missing a beat on the computer.)* I'm sorry you have to wait, sir — we're awful busy this morning.

MAN. We don't even have our juice! I don't even see our waitress!

GAIL. She's in the kitchen, looking after your special order.

MAN. You sure?

GAIL. Positive. Making you happy, that's what we're about.

MAN. ... Better get there soon. *(Man sits. Gail has a headache. Barbara enters clutching laden tray with both hands. The juices are on the tray.)*

GAIL. Balance your tray! *(She spreads the load.)*

BARBARA. He was nice about it.

GAIL. I told you, give 'em their juice first. *When* did you say you waited tables?

BARBARA. 1968. I did arm service, not tray.

GAIL. Where you gonna put that — on a customer's head? *(Barbara has no idea.)* One hand for the tray, one hand for the jack. *(Presents a bus stand; Barbara shifts tray to the flat of one hand and takes it.)* No, you're gonna lose it like that ... Up on your fingertips: never on the flat of your hand. Go on.

BARBARA. Tomato, orange, tomato … Daisy Mae, poached; oatmeal; Snuffy, sunny-side up with patty. Blueberry, honey, and maple.

TEENAGER. *(To Barbara.)* This oatmeal's cold.

BARBARA. Would you like me to reheat it?

TEENAGER. Duh.

MAN. I said wheat toast.

BARBARA. I'll change it. Will there be anything else?

WOMAN. Yes. I better not have prunes. I'll have peaches.

BARBARA. *(Spills prunes on woman, to audience.)* This is not my real life!

FLASHBACK #1

Upscale restaurant: Barbara, servers, editor.

Under music: Two conspicuously young, slender, white-jacketed servers enter. One sets restaurant (tablecloth); one changes Barbara to her professional look. Editor enters.

BARBARA. Manhattan. *(Servers seat the two. Under music, Server #1 brings wine, shows Editor the label; Editor nods, Server pours. We land mid-meal, mid-conversation. Barbara is selling an idea.)*

SERVER #2. *(Returns with food.)* Salmon and field greens; mahimahi and roasted seasonal vegetables. *(Barbara and Editor nod their thanks.)*

EDITOR. Perhaps you haven't heard, we see ourselves as a highbrow rag? We don't give a lot of space to sports.

BARBARA. It's not the sport that interests me, it's the Superbowl: as pseudo — or maybe, neo — ecstatic festival. *(This fails to connect. He waits.)* Did you know that until the thirteenth century, Europeans danced in church? *(He didn't know, and doesn't see the connection.)* Then the church — and the nation state — made us sit down and shut up. They replaced festival — which bonds us to the people around us — with spectacle: the Mass, the military parade. And now, football. But football fans are constantly inventing new rituals of participation that turn spectacle back into festival! What if face paint, and tailgate parties, and giant foam hands express the same desire in the group mind as a peace march — to rebuild the Maypoles and relight the solstice bonfires?

EDITOR. Fascinating idea. For a book. I need something you can nail in five thousand words.

BARBARA. How's this: the real Gulf War Syndrome — murder. Combine McVeigh with the guys who are shooting their wives, and more Americans have been killed by vets who came back from the Gulf, than died in that war.

EDITOR. An elegant half-page! Five *hundred* words.

BARBARA. What's that, five hundred dollars?

EDITOR. Six.

BARBARA. I have a mortgage! ... Welfare moms, being made to walk the plank.

EDITOR. Last month, we profiled three.

BARBARA. Out of four million! Four million women struggling to raise kids, who we're "rescuing from dependency" by booting them into the labor market to scramble for dead-end jobs that pay max, seven dollars an hour. No health care, no child care. What happens to them?

EDITOR. Done to death. *(As Server brings the check, Editor hands her his credit card.)*

BARBARA. God forbid anyone should commit old-fashioned journalism. Get somebody to go out there and try it! Go change beds in a Motel 6, go stock shelves at K-mart, and try to house and feed her kids on the wages.

EDITOR. A woman of high estate sets forth in lowly disguise ... a dramatic reversal of fortune ...

BARBARA. Except no middle-class writer's going to expose *her* children for a month to the conditions poor kids always live in. Fine, make it easier: Subtract the child variable. Just see if she can house and feed *herself.*

EDITOR. When did you want to start?

BARBARA. ... *Oh no. (Server brings tab and card, Editor signs, all exchange nods and smiles.)* I meant somebody younger. *(As they gather their things.)* With good knees.

EDITOR. Hm ... You could be right. And ... It should probably be someone from a working class background, who could pass, not the much-lauded author of a dozen books.

BARBARA. Oh, a "much-lauded author" can't have a working

class background? A working class person can't write books? I don't need to "pass"! My father barely made it out of the copper mines! I was married seventeen years to a warehouseman — an organizer for the Teamsters!

EDITOR. Let's say first draft by June. *(He starts off.)*

BARBARA. I know how hard it is! I won't be surprised enough! You need someone who's gonna be shocked!

FLASHBACK #2

Key West.

BARBARA. *(To audience.)* Hi. My name's Barbara. In real life, I'm a social critic. I'm driven by moral outrage, and curiosity, to speculate, in books and magazines, on what makes humans devour their own kind. This is not the field of research I had in view, when I got my Ph.D. in biology. Blame family history, and the Vietnam War. I'm a radical. I'm not a *post*-feminist. This is not my real hair color. I'm fifty-five years old, but I go to the gym. So. Can a single female — fit, and of reasonable intelligence — land in a strange town, find a place to live and a crappy job, hold the job for a month, eat, keep her clothes clean, and save enough to make next month's rent? This assignment would land most writers I know on a strange planet, the working class. Not strange to this girl. But the man I live with thinks I'm unqualified.

BOYFRIEND. *(Appears; he is a fiction writer.)* You have a famous name, a bank account, an IRA, a house, and you think you can stand in poor people's shoes?

BARBARA. I think I can see how they fit. *(Boyfriend disappears.)* My children insist I could do the research without leaving home.

DAUGHTER. *(Appears; she is a lawyer.)* What do you think you're going to learn, that you couldn't find out on the Net?

BARBARA. *I don't know:* That's how it is in science. Thirty percent of Americans get by on eight dollars an hour or less: Possibly I'll find out how they do it. *(Daughter crosses off.)* The Winn-Dixie supermarket in Key West, near where I really live. I'm giving myself an easy start. I'm being interviewed by a computer. "There are no right or wrong answers. Just pick the first response that comes to mind." … "Strongly Disagree; Moderately Disagree; Moderately Agree; Strongly Agree: *It's all right to be late if you have a good excuse.*" *(Sharing her amusement with the audience.)* "Strongly Disagree." *"A co-worker observed stealing may need the money and should be forgiven."* … "Strongly Disagree." *"Management is responsible for my safety on the job."* Whoa, sneaky, management should care whether workers live or die? "Strongly Disagree!" *"Marijuana is the same as a drink."* … Chemically? Morally? … "Strongly Disagree." *"Some people work better when they're a little bit high."* … "Strongly Disagree." *"There is room in every corporation for a nonconformist."* … "Strongly Disagree." *"I am an honest person."* … who'll tell a lie only to serve the greater good. "Strongly Agree." *(Hits "send.")* Think I passed? Now all I have to do is not shoot off my mouth in some Marxist rant and blow it. *(Waits. No one comes.)* The place to live took a few days: In Key West, you compete with tourists for housing. When I started looking, I didn't know "trailer trash" would become a title I'd aspire to. My new home's eight feet wide; when I sit on the toilet my knees scrape the shower stall, and the rent is 625 dollars a month. Rent, we all learned in school, should be a quarter of your income and then you'll be fine. At that rate, I need to make fifteen dollars an hour. But it's my own little castle. I brought every book I've been wanting to read. *(Waits. No one comes.)* I made safety rules: One: I'll always have a car; two, homelessness isn't an option: If it comes to that, we dump the experiment; three, if the next meal's ever in question, I dig out my ATM card and cheat … Does a live human ever appear? … Maybe I should've used my maiden name. If there's a human, what if they read *Harper's*? … This T-shirt — L.L. Bean, for God's sake. What was I thinking? … The shoes! — What entry-level worker buys Reeboks?

MANAGER. *(Enters with Barbara's printout.)* So … Barbara.

BARBARA. *(Suddenly humble.)* Hi.

MANAGER. *(Looking from the form to her face.)* It's been a while since you held a job.

BARBARA. *(To audience.)* For the greater good — *(To Manager.)* — I stayed home as long as my children were in school.

MANAGER. "Divorced" … Live alone?

BARBARA. I do now.

MANAGER. But not in Key West.

BARBARA. No, but just up the road.

MANAGER. You have a car ...

BARBARA. Yes.

MANAGER. Insurance?

BARBARA. Yes.

MANAGER. And you're willing to work nights.

BARBARA. Anytime, it makes no difference.

MANAGER. Ever been fired?

BARBARA. No, uh-uh.

MANAGER. Why is that?

BARBARA. I guess I'm pretty cooperative.

MANAGER. Ever steal anything from any employer?

BARBARA. No.

MANAGER. Ever file a fraudulent medical claim?

BARBARA. No.

MANAGER. *(With studied casualness.)* Ever belong to a union?

BARBARA. My ex-husband did ... They took his money and never did anything!

MANAGER. Okay. Be here Monday at six A.M.

BARBARA. Really? That's it?

MANAGER. Long as you pass the drug test.

BARBARA. ... You haven't told me the pay.

MANAGER. Six-twenty an hour. *(Hands her a paper cup.)* Take this to room twelve, they'll tell you what to do. We'll let you know the results. *(Manager exits.)*

BARBARA. In your dreams! I'm gonna squat down and pee in a cup — probably in front of a surveillance camera — for six dollars and change an hour ... *(Calculates.)* ... 240 dollars a week? Not to mention — marijuana may leave traces after thirty-plus years of use. Takes months to break down: It's not water-soluble. *(Hands cup to audience member.)* You can keep this, it's a long show. *(Takes want ads from purse and strides to phone.)* ... Hello, I'm Barbara, I interviewed today for your housekeeping job ... Oh. Well, thank you, but I'm not looking for waitress work ... *(To audience.)* Left me bone-tired when I was eighteen. *(Makes another call.)* Hello, you're advertising for housekeepers? ... Check back when? ... Thank you. *(Makes another call.)* Hello, I saw your ad for housekeepers? ... No, just English ... Okay, thanks, but I'd rather not waitress. *(To audience.)* I'm on the wrong end of an ethnic equation. White skin has to wait tables; dark skin gets to scrub floors.

Scene 2

Kenny's, $2.15 per hr. Four P.M. the same day, in the locker room: George, Hector, Gail, Barbara, Philip, Joan.

George enters with a tray of dirty dishes, hurriedly lights a cigarette, takes a long drag.

HECTOR. *(Off.)* George! *(George carefully places burning cigarette in ashtray, exits. Hector enters, takes a long drag, places burning cigarette carefully in ashtray, exits. Barbara enters.)*

BARBARA. In there's our kitchen. Call it Kenny's stomach. The floor's slick with spilled food — we all walk like this. *(Little steps, as if in shackles.)* Our sinks: clogged with decomposing lettuce scraps and lemon wedges; our counters: tacky with yesterday's syrup. Over there's the garbage and dish room: Call that the lower intestine. *(George enters, retrieves cigarette, takes a long drag.)*

GAIL. *(Off.)* George! *(George hands cigarette to Barbara, exits.)*

BARBARA. *(Hunting for ashtray.)* Almost the shift change, after the lunch rush. Philip has asked me to wait. *(Puts out cigarette.)* Notice the pay? The law assumes servers live on tips. Restaurants only have to make up the difference between your tips, and minimum wage. *(George enters with tray of clean dishes, goes for cigarette, finds it put out.)*

GEORGE. Barbara — no, no! *(He exits.)*

BARBARA. I take too long to catch on — Philip's probably gonna fire me. You're about to observe, in his natural setting, the low-wage worker's nearest predator: the manager. *(Philip enters.)*

PHILIP. Barbara. I have a question for you.

BARBARA. Yes?

PHILIP. Does the company pay for idleness?

BARBARA. ... Sorry?

PHILIP. Earlier, I saw you sitting down. And you were not wrapping silverware.

BARBARA. I didn't have any tables ... I'd done my side work ...

PHILIP. Side work is never done. Should I have to tell you, "Wipe down the dessert case, vacuum the dining room"?

BARBARA. … Not again.

PHILIP. Please do not judge our standards by some lax behavior you may see: waitresses gossiping, kitchen staff sneaking a cigarette. This place was anarchy when I came on board, but we are going to have better discipline. Two rolls, four butter patties, handfuls of croutons! The rule is one roll, two butters per customer, six croutons per salad! *(Offstage, dishes crash.)*

HECTOR. *(Off.)* ¡Puñeta! ¡Me cago en la madre del jodido plato!

PHILIP. That will cost him a fine. Now. You roll seventy-five sets of silverware before the start of each shift.

BARBARA. Befo — ?

PHILIP. Standard for the industry. And: I did not like to embarrass you by mentioning this on the floor. But we also have standards for grooming. Tomorrow, kindly wear your hair in a net. *(Philip exits.)*

BARBARA. … Why did I take that? *(George and Gail limp on, light cigarettes, start changing. Gail's head is killing her.)*

BARBARA. How much should I — *(She indicates George.)*

GAIL. How'd you do?

BARBARA. Twenty-two dollars.

GAIL. Give 'im three. *(Hector enters.)* I'll take care of Hector for you.

BARBARA. We tip the cooks, too?

GAIL. You wanna get your special orders. *(Barbara starts to get money out.)* Just today — it'll get better. *(Pays George.)* Dream of me. *(He smiles and nods thanks. She turns to Hector, pays him.)*

HECTOR. Gailie!

GAIL. For her, too.

HECTOR. Oh.

BARBARA. *(To George.)* You saved my life today: Thank you.

GEORGE. *(Accepting money.)* Thank you … I no … English. I … *(Offers pack.)* Cigarette?

BARBARA. Thanks: I'm trying to quit.

GEORGE. Ah! I quit too. *(Offers.)*

BARBARA. What the hell? *(She takes one and he lights it for her.)*

GEORGE. I … America … seven days.

BARBARA. From … *(He looks blank.)* You … what country?

GEORGE. Ah! Czech.

BARBARA. Czech Republic, or Slovakia?

GEORGE. Republic, yes! *(Joan enters, stylish in black dress and high heels.)*

JOAN. Okay, everybody — party time in the salt mines! *(Gail,*

Hector, George mumble hello.) What's Philip's new rule for today?
GEORGE. *(At a cue from Hector, who has rehearsed him.)* "Go fuck yourself, Philip." *(General applause.)*
JOAN. All right! *(To Hector.)* Hi, my Chiquito Banano — what're we gonna do when he says, "No Sex in the Kitchen"?
HECTOR. Oh, Joanie, *te muestro un "banano" bien bonito?*
JOAN. *(Waving off the alcohol fumes.)* Hoo — bottle that and start your own label. Georgie, you know bad ol' Gail wants into your pants. But don't you worry, I'm not gonna let her. *(Gail groans.)* You got that migraine again. I got ibuprofen. *(Getting pills out.)* Hey, all: I got a new address: Day's Inn! *(To Barbara.)* Hi, I'm Joan.
GAIL. This's Barbara — still with us after her first day. This's Joan, the dinner hostess.
JOAN. Happens every time she don't get her estrogen. *(Joan ministers to Gail.)*
HECTOR. *(Beckoning to George.) Eh, puta!*
GEORGE. Yes?
HECTOR. *Pato.*
GEORGE. Yes.
HECTOR. *Maricon — nos vamos.*
GEORGE. *Vamos!* Okay! Yes! Goodbye! *(He exits.)*
HECTOR. Can say anything: He don' speak Spanish. *(He exits.)*
JOAN. Four months in this dump and still not on the health plan, 'cause they "lost her forms." And *this'd* give you a headache — she shares a room with a guy, and he's started hittin' on her every night. *(To Gail.)* Toldja you oughta do like me!
BARBARA. You live at Day's Inn?
JOAN. Hell, no — I live in my van. Car payment's the cheapest rent I ever found. Hundred eighty-six dollars! That's a month, not a week.
BARBARA. You don't look like you live in a van.
JOAN. *(Models her dress.)* Seven bucks at Salvation Army. Met me yesterday, I'da *smelled* like I live in a van. But now the manager at Day's Inn says I can park there, and Marianne, girl that's on nights, and her boyfriend live there for real, so I can shower anytime I want!
BARBARA. Wait — she works here, and they pay sixty bucks a night at Days' Inn? That's something I don't understand — why anyone would live in a motel. I found a nice clean trailer, hooked up, with a kitchen, for 625 a month.
GAIL. ... Where'd you get the deposit?
BARBARA. *(To audience.)* I could tell the truth: "I'm an imposter.

I started my low-wage life with a slush fund of twelve hundred dollars." But — for the greater good — I lie. *(To them.)* From my second ex-husband!

JOAN and GAIL. *(Approve with high-fives.)* Girlfriend! *(They exit opposite ways.)*

BARBARA. I thought low-wage workers must know secret economies that let you get by on bad pay. Wrong. The less you have, the more everything costs you.

Scene 3

K-mart: Barbara, cashier, stockboy; onstage, checkout counter. Barbara arrives with shopping cart containing: soup pot, pint-sized sauce pan, two cans of Progresso soup, wooden spoon, bag of lentils, jar of bay leaves.

CASHIER. *(Running the bar codes.)* 8.99 ... 5.99 ... 2.49 ...

BARBARA. For a spoon?

CASHIER. Codes don't lie. Coulda gotten a plastic one. 1.49, 2.29, .89, .99, 2.29, 3.49, 11.99 ...

BARBARA. *(Conscious a line is forming behind her.)* Could you add that up?

CASHIER. ... 44.59.

BARBARA. ... Without the tea kettle? *(She starts to take it back.)*

CASHIER. I have to scan that ... 32.70 ...

BARBARA. Without the soup pot.

CASHIER. There's people behind you.

BARBARA. *(To the line.)* I'm sorry — I have to rethink this.

CASHIER. *(On mike.)* Samantha, we're gonna need a re-shelver out front.

OFFSTAGE VOICE. *(On mike.)* Dylan, we need you on 9. *(Barbara puts an edited selection of items on counter. Stockboy enters, disgusted.)*

CASHIER. 5.99 ... 1.49 ... 2.99 ... 2.99 ... you still want these lentils and bay leaf?

BARBARA. Guess not.

CASHIER. Comes to 15.26. *(Barbara pays.)* Cover that on your tips and still put gas in your car. I used to work at Kenny's. *(Stockboy wheels off the cart of discarded items.)*

Scene 4

Kenny's, $2.15 per hour. Barbara, Gail.

The two sit rolling silverware. Barbara wears a hairnet.

GAIL. Wait. He's good lookin', good in bed, and makes good money. What the hell are you doing here?

BARBARA. Trying to make a living.

GAIL. Wanna do that in Key West, come in wintertime, tourist season. Seventy, seventy-five a night. Then get out before summer: not get stuck here, like me. I keep thinkin' about Arizona: That's where my youngest son is. But my car'd never make it halfway. Needs an alternator, Earl always said. I'm tryin' to talk Joan into us goin' in her van: Her daughter moved to California. But Joan's the kind that sticks to a place. Joanie's not a tumbleweed like me.

BARBARA. She has a grown daughter?

GAIL. Twenty-five, I think. My big son's thirty-two. He's in Waukesha, Wisconsin. Just saying that I get the shivers. I gotta be someplace warm.

BARBARA. Somehow I didn't think of you as having kids.

GAIL. Somehow I didn't either. Both of 'em grew up with their dads: I kept on meetin' someone else who looked better. But I got grandbabies I'd like to see.

BARBARA. Seventy a night, I could save enough. Thirty only comes to a hundred and fifty ... salary a whole eighty-six dollars — I won't make my rent.

GAIL. ... Think you can use somebody to share that trailer?

BARBARA. Two people'd have to take turns breathing!

GAIL. I kill that sex fiend, it's your fault. Well — ask Nita if there's an opening where she does welding ... phone sales, used to be good ... Had a computer, now, you could work at home ... Tampa, I did real good with Avon on the side, but that's gotta be someplace people know ya.

BARBARA. Are you serious: Two shifts here and then go do another job?

GAIL. Where've *you* been the last twenty years?

Scene 5

Economy Inn, $6.10 per hour. D-day begins: Barbara, Carlie.

Carlie and Barbara let themselves into a room, hauling a cleaning cart.

BARBARA. This hotel's attached to Kenny's. I hounded the manager not to discriminate. Six hours here, times five days will make 183, plus 250 from Kenny's; two jobs is gonna make everything work. 433 dollars a week.

CARLIE. Hold up. *(Searches for tips, finds none.)* Millie? Harcourt takin' our tips again …

BARBARA. She's talking about one of the managers.

CARLIE. You have eight as a stayover and it's a checkout. That makes fifteen — out of nineteen rooms. *(Listens disgustedly. Hangs up.)* So make up the motherfucker.

BARBARA. Her name's Carlie. *(The two perform the following routine. Barbara, pushing to finish early, works briskly; Carlie works at a languid pace. She suffers from foot and joint pain and wears cheap, thin-soled sneakers. Barbara, in room: strips and remakes the bed. Dusts and wipes down the headboard, TV. Carlie, in bathroom: dumps dirty towels in corridor for pickup. Keeps one large dirty towel to clean with. Wipes down the tub, toilet, and then the sink, all with the same towel. Both must cross to and from the cart, and can observe each other's work styles.)*

CARLIE. That's all I need — a White Tornado. Miss Fitness, prob'ly go to the gym. Ever *had* an ass, maybe that's where she left it. Want to make sure I see how fast she can go. We both gonna see how long she can keep it up. She's definitely said goodbye to fifty.

BARBARA. Moves like she's underwater! The slow-motion stroll. "I'm hauling 200 pounds around — you expect me to do more than that?" I wonder how old she is? She's missing most of her teeth! *(Finds a package on cart.)* Hot dog rolls?

CARLIE. That's mine! *(Barbara puts it back. They move to another room. Barbara works at the same athletic pace.)* Somebody payin' you by the room?

BARBARA. I'm sorry?

CARLIE. Don't rush me. We both bein' paid by the hour.

BARBARA. *(Stung.)* I'm *really* sorry — I didn't think — I have to leave by four to get to my other job.

CARLIE. You can leave: Rooms'll still be here ... Whole lotta gunk on that floor. *(Barbara now carefully keeps Carlie's pace. It's not difficult: She's getting tired.)*

BARBARA. You work fast, you earn less ... Yeah, but: can't be long till time and motion studies catch up with *that.* And then how long is she gonna last? She's not faking that joint pain. And her sneakers have quarter-inch soles! Her feet have gotta be screaming by now. I wonder how many years she's been doing this? *(They move to another room.)*

CARLIE. Why did I open my mouth? She prob'ly a spy. Like that one they sent last week, creepin' up behind folks, writin' down times. Or maybe, she a *plant:* They put her here to prove how fast it can get done, then the other one gon' come with her notebook. I know somep'm bout this one ain't right. Them Reeboks she wearin' cost sixty-four dollars. *(Picks up Barbara's sandwich.)* Hmh — turkey and cheese. She a spy, all right.

BARBARA. Oh! God! Ugh! *(She must dispose of a used condom, which is almost too much for her.)* Ugh — I touched — yuk! *(Sprays disinfectant on her hand.)* How can people — ugh! Don't these people have any shame?

CARLIE. In fronta who — us? Pass you in the hallway, act like you not even alive. Till something get stolen, or they don't like how you do your job — then they're all over you. *(Retrieves the hot dog rolls, sits.)* Lunch break! *(Clicks on TV.)*

TV HEROINE VOICE. You don't understand, Helen — I'll always love Eric! I'll never give him up!

TV VILLAINESS VOICE. Then you'll never get out of debt. Break up with him. I'll give you ten thousand dollars.

CARLIE. *(With a world of experience in her advice.)* You take it, girl — I would. *(Barbara is very glad to sit. Opens her sandwich as Carlie bites into a hot dog roll.)*

BARBARA. *(To audience.)* That's her lunch! Okay, I'm shocked.

26

Scene 6

Kenny's, $2.15 an hour plus tips. Barbara, George, Gail, Hector, Joan, Philip, customer. Sign: "Hours later."

Barbara enters with tray. George enters with tray of dirty dishes.

GEORGE. Good evening, Barbara.
BARBARA. Good evening, George.
GEORGE. How are you feeling?
BARBARA. Nine hours on my feet, minus time spent on my knees — *(He looks blank.)* — I am feeling okay. Did you do your homework?
GEORGE. Yes, I do.
BARBARA. Yes, you did.
GEORGE. *(With effort.)* *Whose* teacher are you?
BARBARA. I am *your* teacher. Very good! *(Barbara exits. Philip enters.)*
GEORGE. "Did you do? Yes, I did." *(Joan hurries across with take-out orders.)*
PHILIP. George, please come with me. *(Philip exits. George knows he is busted. He follows. In the kitchen: Hector working, Gail furiously cutting mushrooms.)*
GAIL. Next thing, wait staff'll be *growing* the salad! You guys are s'posed to set us up!
HECTOR. I tol' you, Jesus don' come in today! How the fuck I can do salad prep? "Mash potatoes, no gravy — sour cream!" E'rybody give me fucking special orders! *(Machine spits out order. Hector takes a swig of vodka from a half-pint bottle. Hits bell.)* Pick up Four.
GAIL. *(Chopping tomatoes.)* Barbara's ... *(Barbara enters.)*
BARBARA. Hector, on Eight, that's baked, no fries on the Cary; no potatoes on the John Wayne; rare on the Lana and the Marilyn with tomatoes, no fruit.
HECTOR. Who the fuck needs five special orders?
BARBARA. Five no-tippers in "Love Jesus" T-shirts. I need eight salads.

27

GAIL. Grab a knife, help yourself! A kid could change beds all day, then work the dinner shift — you ain't no kid.

BARBARA. I'll be okay.

HECTOR. Pick up Four! Pick up Nine! *(Gail loads her tray. Barbara rubs her feet.)* Pick up Four!

BARBARA. Oh, God. *(Gail loads Barbara's plates.)*

GAIL. Sit tight: I got it. *(She exits with both orders. Joan enters.)*

JOAN. Ready on that take-out?

HECTOR. Joanie, baby: When we goin' to ran away?

JOAN. I don't need that right now. *(Gail enters, returning one plate.)*

GAIL. On four, the guy wanted mashed, not baked.

BARBARA. Oh, I'm sorry!

GAIL. Joan. Tell me.

HECTOR. Pick up Six. Pick up Six! Barbara!

BARBARA. Oh, God. *(Exits with order.)*

HECTOR. Take-out up.

JOAN. *(Bagging takeout order.)* Scary as hell. Scarier — it come out of nowhere. I wake up, someone's scratchin' on the door by my head: "Hey, baby, lemme in, take me for a ride." Then he's whisperin' what parts of me he wants to eat.

GAIL. Ah, shit.

HECTOR. Pick up Five!

JOAN. Then he musta grabbed the bumper. *(Barbara enters, rocky.)*

BARBARA. Hector, I entered Well on the Wayne, but it's Rare.

HECTOR. What the fuck!

BARBARA. I'm sorry — I'm kinda losing it. *(Philip enters.)*

PHILIP. Everyone! May I have your attention, please? We have an emergency.

GAIL. You ain't kidding — where the hell's Nita?

PHILIP. Her daughter is sick. When *my* child is sick, do I stay at home? But never mind. Hector, please stop and listen. All right, here is the situation: You will find the dry storage room locked.

GAIL/BARBARA. When we're shorthanded? / Then what do we — *(They stop, exasperated.)*

PHILIP. One of the bussers was caught stealing. *(Pauses for dramatic effect.)* Unfortunately, the person must continue working till I can replace him. He is working this shift.

BARBARA and GAIL. *George?*

PHILIP. No need to mention names.

BARBARA. *(To audience.)* I live for this kind of moment. I stand up for the underdog. I take the workers' side. I was raised on stories

28

of ancestors — miners and railroad workers — who looked the boss straight in the eye, and took no crap! *(Starts for Philip, who stares her down. She looks at others, who look at the ceiling. Nobody speaks.)*

PHILIP. When you need supplies, I have the key. *(Computer spits out three orders; Hector yanks them. Then five more as George enters with a load of dirty dishes.)*

GEORGE. Comin' t'rough! *(He stops as everyone stares; he understands they've been talking about him. Philip exits importantly. Hector takes a swig. Barbara tries to find something to say, George wards her off, shaking his head; squeezes past Gail and exits. Offstage, dishes crash.)*

BARBARA. *(To audience.)* I'll give him all my tips after. *(To Gail.)* Why do you stay here?

GAIL. Same reason as you — where else hires you past forty? *(Hector hits bell. Dishing up Gail's order:)*

HECTOR. Pick up Two.

BARBARA. Two — oh, God. *(She grabs tray and loads the dinners.)*

HECTOR. *(Hits bell.)* Pick up Six! Pick up Seven!

BARBARA. "Six" … *(She loads #2 as Gail loads #7. George enters from dish room with tray of clean glasses.)*

GEORGE. Comin' t'rough! *(All three head for the door and collide as Joan enters.)*

JOAN. Code blue, y'all! Tour bus unloading! *(All groan and protest at once:)*

HECTOR. I'm all alone here! GEORGE. I need help!

BARBARA. I have two tables waiting for dinner!

GAIL. Nobody did salad prep! *(Barbara, Gail and George exit with loads. Joan follows them out.)*

JOAN. Barbara, Gail needs help up front! George, you're gonna need fifty setups. I'll take the middle aisle! *(Hector takes a big swig, muttering. Starts dishing the three dinners for number seven. He is starting to lose it: makes a mistake on the second one and has to dump it; furiously flings food on the third. Hits bell.)*

HECTOR. Pick up Nine! *(He starts on the five dinners for number eight. Barbara enters with returned order.)*

BARBARA. Hector, I'm sorry — this one dimwit complained that her mashed were cold, then they all sent 'em back 'cause she said "Let's start together" —

HECTOR. All these? *Your orders.* (He snatches the returns back, slams them into the microwave.)

BARBARA. They haven't had salad yet! *(She chops, flings salads together.)*

GEORGE. Comin' t'rough! *(Crosses with the dirty dishes. With each exit and entrance, he grows angrier. Barbara has to stop and step aside for him. Offstage, dishes crash, dishwasher yells.)*

HECTOR. *(Hits bell.)* Pick up Two! *(Grabs plates out of microwave, hits bell.)* Pick up Four!

BARBARA. *(Flinging salads together.)* … Gotta get their salads out … *(Computer starts printing out fifty orders. It does not stop till end of the scene.)*

HECTOR. Motherfuck! *(Starts on the new orders.)* How I suppose to get fifty orders!? *(Barbara starts to exit with her salads. Gail enters, breathless.)*

GAIL. Great! *(Takes the tray.)* Okay — we still need … forty-two.

BARBARA. Those are m —

GAIL. Just leave 'em bare — put the dressings out on the tables! *(Gail exits. Barbara starts over.)*

HECTOR. *(Hits bell twice.)* Pick up Forty! Pick up Twenty! *(Dishing dinners as orders pile up, yells at computer.)* Shut up, fucking robot machine! *(Pounds bell.)* Pick up Sixty! What the fuck! *(Needing room.)* Pick up Two, Four, Six, Eight! *Barbara!*

BARBARA. … Soon as I serve these salads … *(She starts off with them. Joan enters.)*

JOAN. Okay! *(Takes the salads.)* Now we need … thirty-four!

BARBARA. Those are mine!

JOAN. You can leave 'em bare: Just put the dressings out! *(Joan exits. Barbara starts over.)*

GEORGE. Comin' t'rough! *(He crosses with tray of clean plates, again forcing her aside.)*

HECTOR. *(Hits bell.)* Pick up Ten. *(Shuffling plates to make room. Gail enters.)*

GAIL. Barbara, we need those dressings — *(Sees salads.)* I told you to leave 'em bare! *(Takes them.)*

BARBARA. *(Holding onto the tray.)* Gimme those salads!

HECTOR. *(Pounds bell.)* Pick up Twenty-seven! *(Finds no more room.)* Pick up Ten, Twenty, Forty, Sixty! *(Empties bottle.)*

GAIL. *(Sees the piled-up orders.)* Barbara!

HECTOR. Pick up fucking Two and Four! Pick up fucking Six, pick up fucking Eight!!!

GAIL. Barbara?

HECTOR. *(Dishing dinners, shuffling plates.)* Barbara! *(Philip enters.)*

PHILIP. Barbara! I have three tables that all belong to one waitress, that haven't even gotten their salad! *(Barbara comes to consciousness of the mess she has made. Joan enters.)*

30

JOAN. Hector, how we doing on those dinners?

HECTOR. How many you want? *(Throws one at her. Customer bursts in.)*

CUSTOMER. I want to speak to the manager!

JOAN. *(Wiping food off her face.)* Sir, he's right here.

CUSTOMER. We've been waiting twenty-five minutes for our food!

PHILIP. I'm very sorry, sir. I believe this is your order. If you will kindly go back to your table, I will personally serve your dinners, and your salads.

CUSTOMER. Whattayagonna do about this idiot waitress?

BARBARA. *(As all stare at her, to audience.)* I leave. *(She does, like a zombie. Gail steps into her path; then out of it. All watch her off, then:)*

GAIL. Okay, let's get this show on the road. *(All turn their backs and go back to work.)*

BARBARA. Strangely, the door opens when I push it, the thick tropical night air parts and lets me pass ... I don't feel vindicated. No "Fuck you" surge of relief. I just ran out on friends. I grabbed for my privilege. Millions of Americans get up in the morning and go to two jobs this hard, every day — and I copped out the first time I tried.

And why didn't I stand up for George?! ... I didn't even remember to give him my tips!

The next night ... *(Gail enters, leaving work.)*

BARBARA. P-s-s-t — ! Gail!

GAIL. I was wondering if we'd see you again.

BARBARA. I have something to confess. I'm not a waitress.

GAIL. I noticed that.

BARBARA. I'm a writer.

GAIL. Hmh.

BARBARA. I'm writing about restaurant work for a magazine. *(She expects Gail to be impressed, but Gail feels she has been used.)* I'm going to tell how hard it is, and how good at it *you* are, and the lousy pay and the no breaks and the filthy kitchen and Philip.

GAIL. That part I'd like to read. *(She starts off.)*

BARBARA. Here. The keys to my trailer. Rent's due on the fifteenth. I transferred the deposit to your name.

GAIL. Wow. *(Barbara expects a hug, or a handshake.)* We're even. *(She exits.)*

End of Act One

31

INTERLUDE

Key West: Barbara and Boyfriend at bus station, with her suitcase.

BOYFRIEND. This is what you call "relationship therapy"? You said *one month!* Admit this much: You're writing about a middle-class woman, on a trip.

VOICEOVER. Attention, Greyhound passengers. Bus Number 32 now boarding for Jacksonville, Charlotte, and Washington, D.C. *(Barbara admits nothing.)*

BOYFRIEND. You don't know what real workers experience. You've got an out. The anthropologist parachutes in, and assumes she can speak for the natives.

BARBARA. It's worse than I thought, and a lot of people have no idea. *(Kisses him.)* I need three trips. I'm going to make this a book. *(Boyfriend exits.)* I was raised to try, try again. I can do this. I was blindsided — all around. This time I know what to watch out for.

VOICEOVER. Bus Number 65 now boarding for Augusta, Waterville and Bangor ... Bus Number 65 now loading out of Door Number 4.

BARBARA. I picked Maine, for its whiteness. One place a blue-eyed, native English-speaking Caucasian can get a fair shot — you don't have blacks and Latinos and fresh-off-the boat immigrants hogging all the bad jobs and crummy housing.

ACT TWO — MAINE

Scene 1

Projection appears: "Blue Haven Motel, $120/week."
Barbara, still with suitcase, enters a motel room.

BARBARA. A row of tiny white cottages up against the pine trees, ten miles outside of Portland. Twelve-foot square, including bathroom and kitchenette. There's a frying pan, a cereal bowl, a drinking glass and a plate. The TV has cable, till they find out the subscriber's gone.

　　Ever wonder how you'd do if you were lost in the woods? Or if you got amnesia? Say your body and mind were intact, but you've forgotten who you're supposed to be?

Scene 2

Magic Maids, $6.65 per hour. Holly, Barbara, Maddy, Marge; later, Nanny, Rich Lady.

Holly is newly pregnant: bad news which she has told no one. In this scene, she fights morning sickness. Holly enters with cleaning caddy, followed by Barbara, who is adjusting her new uniform.

HOLLY. Okay! Everything we do, we have a system and a product. We're national, you know, so we have high standards. Lots of services don't even train.
BARBARA. I applied to one. They said, "Cleaning is in a woman's bones."

HOLLY. And that helps! But there's still a right and wrong way. Ready? *(Barbara is all attention.)* These are your products, these are your rags. Spray the white one with Windex — *(Barbara obeys, and continues obeying. Holly waves away the fumes.)* — and put it in your left apron pocket. Spray the yellow one with disinfectant, and put it in your middle pocket. Very good! This is the vacuum cleaner. *(Bending to pick it up makes her momentarily dizzy; she covers this with a smile.)* Hoo! Hot today. It goes right on your back, like this. See, now you're the vacuum cleaner.

BARBARA. Whee, I'm a vacuum!

HOLLY. With this kind, there's nothing to trip over, nothing to get in the way. Now, whatever job we're doing, we use the section system. Picture the area you're going to clean divided in sections, big as you can reach. Start in the left-hand corner and clean section by section, left to right, top to bottom.

BARBARA. Clean with what?

HOLLY. With the products.

BARBARA. You don't use any water?

HOLLY. Our products are very scientific. *(Maddy enters and watches.)* Okay, if a floor's really dirty, sometimes you *have* to use water, but just use half a bucket.

BARBARA. My mom would turn over in her grave.

HOLLY. I didn't know my mom.

MADDY. Holly! Think Barbara's ever cleaned house before?

HOLLY. She has to learn the system!

BARBARA. I was asking questions.

MADDY. We're loaded up. *(She exits.)*

HOLLY. Maddy doesn't see why I want to improve myself. Okay, let's go. *(The four load into a car. Holly drives.)*

MARGE. I had such a yen for egg salad today. I had some nice chives to put into it. But you can't bring egg salad in this heat. So what I did, I took black olives, the pitted kind, and I minced 'em up with onion and celery, and plenty of black pepper. Then I tasted it and I thought, "Needs some body." So I —

MADDY. Barbara, you a smoker?

BARBARA. At times.

MADDY. *(To Marge.)* Toldja! That makes three to one. Holly don't smoke.

HOLLY. This is it: Load in. *(In the house, the maids haul in their stuff. They stare around an enormous kitchen. On the counter, a Brita water pitcher and glass.)*

34

BARBARA. A kitchen big as the lab where I did my thesis work. *(She takes out her water bottle and is about to drink.)*
HOLLY. No! There are rules we follow when we're in a house. We don't smoke, we don't swear, we don't chew gum, and we don't eat or drink — anything.
MADDY. *(On phone.)* … That you, Darren? … Honey, can I speak to Darlene? … What do you mean, she's not there? … " "The laundromat!?" Who's watching Tommy and Kimmy? … Thank you, you're a very good boy. Could you put Tommy on, please? *(Holly signals frantically.)* Bye-bye, sweetheart, Mommy loves you but she's got to go. *(She hangs up. Nanny enters, studies the group.)*
NANNY. *(Addresses Barbara.)* Are you in charge?
HOLLY. *I* am!
NANNY. Mrs. Wentworth asked me to remind you: no chemicals in the nursery wing, or on the Kashans.
MADDY. The who?
NANNY. The carpets. Use wood alcohol: You'll find it on the back porch, along with the copper polish for those pots. Here are the rest of the instructions. My name's Vera, I'm Baby's nanny. I'm Number Six on the Intercom: Buzz me if you have any questions.
MADDY. What's wrong with the air conditioning?
NANNY. We leave it off on account of Baby. Oh — if you need to use the facilities, use the one on the service porch. *(She exits.)*
HOLLY. They have five bathrooms. "Move everything on all surfaces." "Be sure to clean undersides of all baseboard molding."
MADDY. Eight miles, or ten?
HOLLY. Maddy, I have to tell you something. Ted's very concerned about your attitude.
MADDY. How does Ted know about my attitude?
BARBARA. *(To audience.)* Ted owns the franchise.
HOLLY. And we're not supposed to use the phone in a house! Okay. Now, Ted wants us to rotate. Maddy, vacuum. *(Maddy straps on the vacuum cleaner.)* Marge, dust. Barbara, kitchen.
MARGE. I don't know … the climbing … my ankles are bad today.
HOLLY. Okay, you do kitchen. Barb —
MARGE. It's a granite floor … that's really hard on my knees.
HOLLY. What am I supposed to do, Marge — Ted wants us to rotate! … Okay, Barbara, kitchen, but when you're done, go straight and help Marge dust. I do bathrooms. 200 minutes. *(Explains to Barbara.)* He gives us longer on a first-timer.
MADDY. Think Baby's Nanny'll make us lemonade? *(Exeunt the*

three. Barbara on her knees, scrubs for a while before she speaks.)
BARBARA. She wasn't kidding, hard on the knees ... sheets of sweat, pouring down my back ... Lost fluids are supposed to get replaced. You don't see a construction guy far from his Gatorade, or a Yuppie from her water bottle ... *(Upstage, Rich Lady enters with glass of iced tea and reclines on chaise lounge by pool.)* Does "Mrs. Wentworth" know her kitchen's a vast obstacle course stretching between me and a tall glass of water? *(Gets up, bracing her knees, and rubs them.)* Oof! *(Crosses to wash panes on French doors.)* That pool is so blue ... how deep? What would happen if I just ran out, and jumped in? ... Down, down, down ... she's looking right at me! As if ... does she recognize me? *(Rich Lady gets up and approaches.)* Oh, my God — she does! I probably spoke at her college! ... Come clean, and swear her to secrecy.
RICH LADY. Are you ... *(Barbara sheepishly acknowledges that she is indeed the celebrated author.)* ... wiping in circles on those windows?
BARBARA. ... I wasn't thinking.
RICH LADY. You need to work at right angles: up, down, left to right. Understand?
BARBARA. I understand. *(She finishes the panes under Rich Lady's watchful eye.)*
RICH LADY. And I'm having a problem with the faucets in the vegetable sink. They keep bleeding rust onto the marble. Could you just scrub extra hard there?
BARBARA. Okay.
RICH LADY. *(Leaving.)* Oh, and do the entryway floor while you're at it? Thanks. *(She waits to see Barbara return to her knees, then returns to her chaise. Maddy enters, checks that Rich Lady's not watching, grabs phone.)*
MADDY. Darlene? What the hell are you doing, leaving my kids alone? ... Oh, like I don't know they're your asshole brother's, too. They're five and three! ... Well, I didn't say it was okay, and I'm the one pays you fifty a week! *(Holly totters in sick to her stomach, drops bucket and half-collapses. Maddy hangs up.)* Holly? Are you okay?
HOLLY. *(Waving her away.)* Fine. I'm just a little nauseous.
MADDY. ... Are you pregnant? ... Holly, answer me ... How far along? ... Here. *(Pours from Brita filter.)* Drink some water. *(Holly refuses.)* You need it — to hell with the rule!
HOLLY. We don't use bad words in a house! *(She pours the water back.)*
MADDY. Jesus!

HOLLY. Maddy! *(Maddy throws up her hands and exits. Barbara pretends to work.)* Are you married?

BARBARA. I quit going that far.

HOLLY. I didn't want to come to work today, but my husband made me. Ooh, I'm like this every morning.

BARBARA. Have you been to the doctor? *(Holly shakes her head.)* Tell your husband — you shouldn't be around all these chemicals.

HOLLY. He doesn't know. He's outta work.

BARBARA. Oh! ... Well ... If you're going to keep doing this job, you have to eat. I saw you at lunch: half a bag of Doritos?

HOLLY. I just can't eat.

BARBARA. Here. Pure Protein bar. I always carry one in case I start seeing spots.

HOLLY. *(Unable to take her eyes off it.)* Oh, no, thanks.

BARBARA. I wont eat it, I'm full.

HOLLY. I couldn't, really.

BARBARA. I had a big fat ham and cheese sandwich. *(Holly takes the bar, moves out of Rich Lady's eyeshot.)*

HOLLY. If you're sure you don't need it — *(Devours it.)* Thanks. Don't say anything to the girls, okay? I want to keep it secret till I tell Ted.

BARBARA. I won't if you promise to tell him today.

HOLLY. I can't! He just made me Team Leader! He gave me a raise! Oooh, just when I was getting to be somebody!

BARBARA. Holly. Ted can't afford to lose you — you're too good. But chemicals are bad for the baby. *(She pours a glass of water, hands it to Holly, and fixes her with an iron gaze till she drinks it.)* Tell him you need to stick to dusting. I'm almost done here — I'm gonna finish the bathrooms.

HOLLY. Oh, no, you can't do that.

BARBARA. I can and I will. *(She pours a glass of water. Freeze Holly as Barbara addresses audience.)* I'll do the work of two people, three if necessary, to defend this poor, probably abused, malnourished kid, who needs some old-fashioned consciousness-raising! ... *(Upstage, Rich Lady exits.)* And that's not rust, lady, staining your marble! That's blood — the blood of the world-wide working class! The people who quarried your marble, loaded it in trucks and on ships, drove nails into hard timber to put up your house and now, sweat and strain and risk their unborn children to clean it! Blood stains this whole house, lady — it stains your entire life! ... Excuse me — was I shrill? It happens sometimes.

(Fills the glass and drinks it triumphantly.) This time I don't cop out, and I don't shut up.

Scene 3

Woodcrest Residential Facility, $7 per hour. Barbara, four ancient patients in wheelchairs; later, Pete.

Four Alzheimer's patients, strapped into wheelchairs. #1 bangs and lolls like a baby who doesn't want to be in the car seat; #2 rocks; #3 sits stone-still and stares; #4 is a dirty old man who keeps grabbing for Barbara. Barbara enters with four breakfast trays.

BARBARA. *(To audience.)* How I spend my weekend, seven A.M. to three. — Two jobs, but spread over seven days. It's worth it: I'm in the chips. Two hundred sixty-six from Magic Maids plus a hundred-twelve from here, the Woodcrest Residential Facility, brings my take-home to...? Add it up: ... three hundred and seventy-eight dollars! Rent's a comfortable forty percent. I could afford to go out to a movie — but every night, I fall into bed. Marguerite, enjoy your breakfast ... Letty, you don't get sugar ... Grace, skim milk, special for you ... John, I'm gonna register you as a sex offender ... *(Filling cups, to audience.)* Decaf. Otherwise things get pretty wild ... Two people didn't come in this morning: I'm feeding the whole ward by myself. Marguerite, no, don't dump your orange juice ... Grace, aren't you going to eat? Letty! You can't have his donut! *(Grace is mumbling.)* What is it, Grace. You want to what? ... *(Grace throws milk on Barbara. All four patients cackle. Pete, in cook's uniform, enters and watches as she cleans up the mess.)*
PETE. Barbara?
BARBARA. *(To audience.)* Pete.
PETE. When you get a break, wanna catch a cigarette outside?
BARBARA. In the rain?
PETE. We can sit in my car.
BARBARA. ... Why not? When I'm done with the dishes. *(He nods and goes. As Barbara talks, she rolls patients off one by one.)* The title is

38

"Dietary Aide," but the job's nine-tenths cleanup and dishwashing. There's supposed to be a Nurse's Aide to move the patients. By the time you've scraped, rinsed, presoaked and stacked forty plates, loaded them, in twenty-pound racks, into a machine that's down here — *(Bends to show where.)* — mopped up the dining room while it runs, then unloaded the racks, it's time for the next meal. But — as someone beginning to be in a position to know — the Woodcrest is not a bad place to work. The manager's straightforward, she's not a neurotic, and she knows how to leave you alone. It's worth noting that in my whole low-wage life, this is the only workplace that's not a corporation. *(Pete, Barbara, sit in a car, smoking.)*

PETE. … Linda's okay, but sometimes she can come down real hard. Got on my case last week 'cause I let a dessert slip — onto some diabetic's tray. What's she think this is, a hospital? Face it, nobody gets out of here alive.

BARBARA. *(To audience.)* What anti-smoking crusaders don't understand: Smoking is an act of self-nurturance, carried out in defiance. Work is what you do for others, smoking's what you do for yourself. At work in America, the only thing a lot of people can call their own is the tumors they're nourishing and the time they steal to feed them.

PETE. I'm only working this job for something to do. Not like I need seven bucks an hour. I hit it big in Atlantic City a few years back. Took the money and made some real good investments. Y'oughta see my phone bill, from calling my broker! I'm a pretty major player in Techs. But you stay home, you get stir-crazy: start to feel like an outcast.

BARBARA. *(To audience.)* Agh. The chemicals I'm saving Holly from are starting to give me a rash.

PETE. This is my beach car. I drive it to work, that way I fit in. I got a Lincoln town car in my garage. But for up here, it's kinda showy. Plus, doesn't really fit my lifestyle. Thinking about selling it, buying an SUV. Lexus 4x4's a beautiful ride. I'd pay cash, I don't like to buy things on time. I need an SUV for outdoors. I'm an outdoorsman. You like canoeing?

BARBARA. I've never been.

PETE. Get a day off, I'll take you. I've canoed all the ponds around here. But I'm thinking of selling my canoe, gettin' a kayak. Or maybe, sell the Lexus and get me a bike. A Harley Fat Boy. *(Fading.)* I used to have a Road King. Did a lotta miles on that bike. Maybe this time I'll get an Indian …

BARBARA. *(Overlapping.)* I have a soft spot for Pete. And, if the truth be told, I'm a bit hungry for human contact. Plus, a cook can make a dietary aide's life easy, or very hard. I don't have the energy to be high-minded on *two* jobs.

Scene 4

Magic Maids, $6.65 per hour. Barbara, Ted.

In another car, Ted is driving and expounding sotto voce.

BARBARA. *(To audience.)* Sitting in cars, listening to men. A lot like being back in college. Meet Ted. You might not guess it to look at him, but this man has charisma! The women repeat his jokes; they glow at his praise. Even Maddy, who doesn't have a good word for anything, doesn't have a bad word to say about Ted. And Holly told me, as confirmation of sainthood, that when work is short, he'll send them to finish their day cleaning his own house — which she reports is "really, really nice." Two weeks in.

TED. ... I offered to drive you today, because I think you and I ought to know each other.

BARBARA. *(Alarmed, to audience.)* If you think Pete wasn't boy-friend material ...

TED. I hear you've been doing terrific work.

BARBARA. I try.

TED. *(Chuckles.)* I'm getting really excellent reports. The thing I especially appreciate's the way you're concerned about Holly.

BARBARA. *(To audience.)* Aha. Yesterday she barfed all over some fancy flowerbed, and I made her go home.

TED. I like that. I like a girl who thinks about more than herself. Takes an interest in the big picture. Kinda person's not easy to find. I'm not surprised, though: I was expecting great things. You made a perfect score on the Acutrac test.

BARBARA. *(To audience.)* Despite the warning it had multiple measures "to detect attempts at 'psyching out' the questionnaire"!

TED. I'm not telling you this just to make you feel good. I'm a guy who thinks ahead. Holly'll be leaving us in a few months, and

I'm gonna need another crackerjack Team Leader. Right here, right now, I'm offering you the job.

BARBARA. Um, I have trouble seeing that far down the road.

TED. Take your time. It would mean a pretty hefty pay increase. Seven-fifty an hour.

BARBARA. Wow: Are you sure you can manage it?

TED. But I'm not gonna wait till then to give you a raise. Starting next week, I'm putting you at ... $6.75.

BARBARA. *(To audience.)* For a split second there, I thought about quitting my weekend job.

TED. I appreciate my gals, I want you to know that: especially the good ones, like you and Holly. But, no matter what you do for people, it seems like there always have to be malcontents, kind that have to poison the atmosphere. Always negative, always complaining. *(Stops the car.)* I don't suppose you've met this type of individual.

BARBARA. *(To audience.)* This is my cue to say "Maddy." *(To him.)* Will Holly be getting maternity leave?

TED. *(Caught by surprise.)* ... Well ... we haven't had that policy ... most girls just quit ... With a baby, that's when your absenteeism problem starts.

BARBARA. What you were saying, though, about appreciation — do you think good people might be easier to find if you raised *everybody's* pay?

TED. Our wages are standard for the industry! These girls don't have to be Einstein — they get mother's hours. They're home by four! *(Under Barbara's unrelenting stare.)* Tell you what, though ... I'll give some thought to this maternity issue, if you give some thought to my offer. Deal?

BARBARA. Deal.

TED. Wouldn't want you to think I'm an ogre. *(Barbara gets out.)*

BARBARA. *(To audience.)* Actually, the word that comes to mind is "pimp."

Scene 5

Magic Maids, $6.75 per hour. Barbara, Holly, Marge, Maddy.

41

Again, the maids load into a house.

HOLLY. I called that clinic you told me. It *is* only ten dollars!
BARBARA. Good!
MADDY. *(On phone.)* Hi, honey, it's Mommy ... Everything okay? ... What's Kimmy doing? ... Good. When she wakes up, don't forget to put a new Pamper on her ... I know you can, you're such a big boy. And give her some applesauce ... I "took away the furniture" so you won't fall ... I know you can't: It's locked ... Because I need you to stay in that room! ... Honey, that's why I gave you the potty chair. I love you. *(She hangs up.)*
BARBARA. *(To audience.)* Maddy's moved out of her sister-in-law's into a motel. Marge and her husband own their house, and their daughter, her three kids, and a niece and nephew live with them. Holly isn't just supporting her husband: She's also taking care of his grandmother. I eavesdrop: It saves me from asking dumb questions.
HOLLY. Maddy, vacuum.
MADDY. I remember *this* bitch.
HOLLY. Maddy!
MADDY. — Beautiful lady. She's the one tries to trap you: likes to leave little piles of dirt under the rugs.
HOLLY. Okay, I better vacuum. You do the kitchen. Marge, you have to dust: Put a rag on a broom. Barbara, bathrooms. A hundred minutes. *(Exeunt the three. Barbara begins scrubbing toilet.)*
BARBARA. *(To audience.)* Let's talk about shit. For those of you who've never cleaned a really dirty toilet — there are three kinds of shit stains. Residual landslides on the inside of toilet bowls; splashback remains on the underside of seats; and the most repulsive: brown crusts inside the rim, where turds hit on their way to the water. These leavings can turn you against your own near and dear — try to grok the unwanted intimacy of scraping up behind strangers.

Tubs and showers, now: There you're picking off pubic hair. Tiny coils, that obstinately adhere to surfaces. The American upper middle class *sheds* at a truly alarming rate.

(If Breakout Scene is cut, cut the following paragraph.) I'll say one thing for myself — I've never hired a cleaning person. Various husbands and partners have badgered me to over the years, but this is just not the relationship I want to have with another human being. In fact I find the idea repugnant. *(Optional breakout scene interrupts:)*

BREAKOUT SCENE (Optional)

Actress # 1 plays Barbara; #3 is Carlie/Melissa; #5 is Hector/ Maddy. Cast other two women as appropriate.

ACTRESS #2. *(Enters.)* Hold on. I'm sorry — I have to say something. *(To audience.)* I just want you to know, I'm embarrassed that she said that!

BARBARA. … Excuse me?

ACTRESS #2. I'm not talking to you, Barbara. I'm talking to [actress' real name]. [Stage manager], can we have the house lights, please? *(Actress #1 signals "don't do it!" but house lights go up.)* Have you ever hired cleaning help? have you?

ACTRESS #1. Occasionally.

ACTRESS #2. *(To audience:)* I am so sick of us being hyprocrites! Because we're saying that anyone who hires cleaning help is like that rich lady in the last act! It's one thing for Barbara: She's a freelance writer, she works at home. I'm almost never home — I *need help! (To audience:)* Who's with me? How many of you have cleaning help? … Look, I promise I won't single you out, I won't haul you up onstage: I'm just taking a poll … come on now, I know the average income of the [insert theatre] subscriber … That's better. And how many of your wives do? … Like me! I have a two-year old. And when I'm in a show, I either rehearse all day or I do eight shows a week. And I refuse to be guilt-tripped for having someone in twice a month, for three hours — someone *I* hire, and pay well, not a service — so I can have one day with my little girl, and not spend every single spare minute doing housework!

ACTRESS #3. Whoa. What do you call "paying well"? How much do you pay her?

ACTRESS #2. *(Proud.)* Fifteen dollars an hour!

ACTRESS #3. Uh huh. Would you scrape shit for that? *(Actress #2 wouldn't. To audience:)* Would *you?*

ACTRESS #1. *(Righteous.)* I pay twenty!

ACTRESS #3. I think twenty's a bit high. I pay seventeen.

ACTRESS #4. Twenty's rock-bottom. *(Others start to object.)* I'm not about to pay less than what I'd do it for! Nobody here's mentioned, people need jobs! I take it as my social responsibility to provide as much work as I can! I can only afford it every month and a half, but I think we should *all* have maids!

ACTRESS #1. We don't "have maids."

ACTRESS #3. We hire cleaning ladies.

ACTRESS #5. *(Who has been listening.)* Can I talk? I've been a cleaning lady.

OTHERS. Really? / You have? / When?

ACTRESS #5. Hello — young Latina? And I bet I'm not the only one here. Who else here has cleaned houses for money? ... *Quien mas ha limpiado casas? (Ad lib:)* How much did you make? ... *(Ad lib responses.)* Okay, those of you who hire cleaners, what do you pay? Fifteen? Twenty? Can I hear some higher numbers? Come on, the dirtiest jobs should get paid the most! Hey, she's cleaning *your* house, she's saving *your* time: Pay her what your time's worth. Let's say twenty-five dollars — plus benefits!

OTHERS. "Benefits"?

ACTRESS #2. Okay, I think we're done here.

STAGE MANAGER. *(On mike.)* Ladies — ladies! can we get back to the play? Places, please. *(Actresses obey.)*

ACTRESS #2. *(Backing offstage.)* I just had to get that out. Thank you for sharing.

Scene 5 (Continued)

BARBARA. *(To audience.)* Meanwhile, back in Maine: *(If Breakout Scene is cut, resume here.)* Agh. *(She scratches.)* What started as a minor rash has turned into full-scale epidermal breakdown. It's torture all day and worse at night: I wake up every two hours and slather on more anti-itch cream from Rite-Aid. "Latex allergy," pronounces Ted, and gives me cotton-lined gloves, to no effect. I should find myself a clinic or the county emergency room: the care options for my adopted social class. But I'm out of my mind with itching! I call a dermatologist I know in Key West, and bludgeon him into phoning up a prescription. It cost thirty dollars — five hours' pay I have to make up. *(Offstage, scream, and sounds of a human and a vacuum cleaner tumbling and landing. Marge enters.)*

MARGE. Holly fell down the stairs! *(Holly enters hopping on one foot as Maddy tries to stop her.)*

MADDY. Holly, stop, sit down … Holly, whatta you trying to prove?

HOLLY. Let me alone — I'm all right!

BARBARA. Is it your ankle, or your knee?

MADDY. It's her knee.

BARBARA. Can I feel it? *(Holly permits Barbara to feel her knee.)* It's already swollen. Can you put weight on it?

HOLLY. A little … *(She tries. It buckles, and the pain is sharp.)*

BARBARA. Somebody get her some ice.

HOLLY. We can't go into the fridge.

BARBARA. I don't care — get some ice! *(Maddy runs off for ice.)*

MARGE. You can't work on that.

BARBARA. You need to go to the hospital. *(Holly shakes her head no.)* For an X-ray. *(Maddy returns with a bag of frozen peas. Barbara applies them.)*

HOLLY. *(Rubbing her knee.)* I couldn't do that to Ted. *(Others express exasperation.)*

MARGE. You oughta get yourself checked.

MADDY. Listen, Holly.

MARGE. You gotta think of the baby.

HOLLY. Only place I got hurt is my knee.

BARBARA. You got hurt at work. If it turns out to be serious, that means you could get Worker's Comp.

MARGE. You listen.

MADDY. *(Overlapping.)* She could?

BARBARA. But you have to report the accident. *(Holly shakes her head.)*

HOLLY. … Ow … ow … ow …

MADDY. Do it, Holly.

BARBARA. Do one thing, at least? Just talk to Ted and tell him.

HOLLY. No! I can't! Barbara, please! *(But, Barbara dials a number and hands the phone to Holly, who refuses to take it.)*

MARGE. Go on, now.

BARBARA. Hello, Ted? Holly needs to speak with you.

HOLLY. … Ted … ow … it's Holly … No, but, I'm sorry — *(The others can't believe their ears.)* … Ow … I did something really dumb. I slipped on the stairs … Oh, no, not really bad … Oh yeah, I can work through it. *(This is too much for Barbara, and also for Maddy and Marge.)* But Barbara's making a big fuss. She made me call. *(Barbara grabs the phone.)*

45

BARBARA. Listen, Ted ... Don't tell me to "calm down" ... A sprained knee, maybe broken. You're putting your money before her health! ... I said, "Don't tell me that." This girl needs an X-ray, and *you* need to pay for it ... Say it one more time, I'm gonna hang up on you — and get the State in to investigate. This is an industrial accident! ... Okay! *(She hangs up.)* And this is a work stoppage. I'm not moving till you agree to go and get help. *(Marge and Maddy are delighted anyone would go this far.)*

HOLLY. Who do you think you are? How dare you, talking about me like that to Ted?

BARBARA. ... How dare I? You want to know? *(She punches a number. Assuming an upper-class voice.)* ... Hello, the Magic Maids? ... Yes, I need a housecleaner: Do you mind telling me what you charge? ... Oh, a team? Well, but what's the price per maid, per hour? ... I'm sorry, could you repeat that? *(Puts phone to Holly's ear.)* ... I see. Thanks, we'll get back to you. *(She hangs up.)*

MADDY. How much?

HOLLY. ... Twenty-five dollars. *(This is news to Marge and Maddy.)*

MADDY. Get out!

BARBARA. A hundred bucks an hour for the four. Seventy-three dollars we put in his pocket, every hour, every day — and he sends us home with two-twenty a week!

HOLLY. ... It doesn't all go in his pocket. He has to buy the supplies ... And pay for the cars! That's a lot of gas. And insurance! He's got a ton of expenses.

BARBARA. I think he can afford to get you an X-ray. Now sit down and put your leg up and let us finish your work for you, or we're going on strike! *(A silence. Barbara has gone too far.)*

MARGE. *(To audience.)* Uh-oh. I seen it coming, the way she's always saying little things about the job. As if I don't know it stinks. And I know something else: I'm not about to spend a month hunting for another one that's gonna stink just as bad. I don't like to hurt her feelings ... I wonder if she's a Communist.

MADDY. I got things to do. I gotta get home.

MARGE. It's true what Holly says: He has expenses. Overhead. I mean, we don't know what all goes into it.

HOLLY. Barbara does. Barbara knows everything. I'm gonna finish my work. *(Holly switches the vacuum on and exits hopping. Maddy and Marge follow her.)*

BARBARA. *(To audience.)* Barbara doesn't know much. *(The four load into the car. Maddy signals Holly "I'll drive.")*

MADDY. *(To audience.)* Barbara don't know I'm on probation. I lose my job, the state takes my kids. *(She drives, chafing; Barbara broods. Strained silence.)*

HOLLY. What you makin' for dinner, tonight, Marge?

MARGE. I'm gonna make a nice meat loaf. I got half a loaf of bread going stale. I'll use that for the binding, and two eggs, and a can of mushroom soup. I used to always put milk in to wet it, but now I like mushroom soup, and you know what gives a zing to it, with all your spices, and it saves chopping? Onion dip, outta the pack. My sister puts —

MADDY. *(To no one in particular.)* I gotta get a cell phone.

MARGE. *(Pause.)* Barbara?

BARBARA. Sorry.

MARGE. You cook much?

BARBARA. I was thinking about Ted.

MARGE. Oh, he's not gonna fire you, don't worry.

BARBARA. Who's worried? There's millions of jobs out there!

MARGE. Don't even think about quitting: We need you! And you can't just leave Ted in the lurch like that.

BARBARA. Ted? Ted can hire anyone that'll turn up sober at 7:30 in the morning!

HOLLY. No, that's not true. Not everyone can get this job. You have to pass the test.

BARBARA. The *Acutrac* test? "I find it hard to stop moods of self-pity — Often, Sometimes, Never?" "True or False: Management and employees will always be in conflict, because they have totally different sets of goals." That test is *bullshit!* It tells them nothing: It just tells *us* who's boss! *Any idiot* can pass that test! *(Dead silence. Maddy stops the car. The three get out, hauling their stuff, and exit.)* Ted doesn't fire me. I make it to the end of the month, but Holly never again speaks to me directly.

End of Act Two

INTERLUDE #2

Key West. Boyfriend enters bedroom.

BOYFRIEND. *(Calling.)* They came! *(He discovers Barbara is not in bed. He calls into bathroom.)* Come out and look! *(Barbara enters in bathrobe, drops onto bed.)* Let it go!

BARBARA. I've been a day-tripper — I've been a dilettante.

BOYFRIEND. So move on. Come on — you gotta see this. You gotta feel this. It's beautiful.

BARBARA. You spent three thousand dollars on a sofa ... Three months' pay.

BOYFRIEND. Not for us! We have a nice life now. Why? We earned it. We can buy nice stuff! *(She shakes her head.)* It's buffalo hide, it'll be here when we're gone! *(She won't come.)* Nobody handed me anything on a plate. I put myself through school. It would have been easier to quit. Would have been easier to quit writing — I didn't always get paid. But I always had a goal.

BARBARA. Putting yourself through school — was that when you were a single mom?

BOYFRIEND. Face it — we're not all equal! Not everyone has the intelligence. Not everybody has talent! *(Barbara despairs.)*

BARBARA. Your grandparents *owned a farm*. Your parents owned a house. Your mother made you do homework!

BOYFRIEND. I've put in seven-day weeks for three decades, but some people don't like to work!

BARBARA. *(Gets up.)* Nobody I met. *(Exits.)*

ACT THREE — MINNESOTA

PROLOGUE

BARBARA. Minneapolis, late summer … From the plane, an endless vista of blue lakes and green trees; on the Web, a shining prospect of $8-an-hour jobs and $400-a-month apartments. I'm looking for a soft landing.

Last chapter. I just need to get through it without being a jerk.

I have a free apartment for a few days, from friends of a friend, so I can put job-hunting first. I'm looking for retail, or factory work: something that keeps you minding your own business. No more waitressing, housekeeping or nursing homes — I don't do well with up-close-and-personal.

A large, aggressively competetive discount chain, whose name we've gone to great lengths to conceal: Mall-mart. *(Place/Wage sign appears with wages a question mark.)*

Scene 1

Mall-mart, $? per hour. Barbara, Howard.

Barbara is waiting for an interview.

BARBARA. I get cold feet on the Personality Test. "Will they buy it if I lie shamelessly on all fifty questions?" So I sprinkle bits of truth here and there. *(Howard enters with printout.)*
HOWARD. Barb, how ya doin'?
BARBARA. "Barbara." Hi.
HOWARD. Now, you did great on the test. I just wanna ask you some questions. "Rules Must be Followed to the Letter at All Times." You "Agree Moderately." Why not "Strongly"?

BARBARA. *(Making it up as she goes along.)* ... I thought about that. But say the rule was, "Stay on the Floor," and then the store caught on fire. I thought there should be a little room for discretion.

HOWARD. "Discretion" ... Okay! How 'bout "There's room in every corporation for a nonconformist"? Why "Moderately" disagree?

BARBARA. ... Say the manager didn't know the store was on fire. You'd want someone who'd take initiative.

HOWARD. "Initiative!" Okay ... Starting to look like this could work! So Barb. What makes you want to join Mall-mart?

BARBARA. ... Well, I like people ... and I love to shop ... I just thought it would be a good fit.

HOWARD. It is, if you're a people person. We think of customers as guests in our house. 'Fact, that's what we call 'em: guests. I know what you're wondering: "How can he think of Mall-mart as "we"? He's talking about the world's largest retailer, that just opened its 10,000th store!" Well Barb, Mall-mart's also a Family. 1.2 million people, close like you wouldn't believe. You probably think "Oh, that family stuff's corny." But you should meet the people that come to our monthly meetings — from all over: Canada, Mexico, Indonesia! I'm gonna tell you the truth. Some of these folks mean more to me than my own brother and sister.

Here, you're not an employee, you're an Associate. I'm not a manager, I'm a People Servant. You're here to serve the Guests, and I'm here to serve you. You know when you said "initiative"? I said, "This lady's lookin' good!" Because part of a People Servant's job, is to inspire our Associates to come up with ideas, and you look like you have a lot of 'em. And if your idea's the best one that month, you'll be honored at the next meeting and we'll bring you there, all expenses paid. *And* you get a share of the profit.

BARBARA. When?

HOWARD. Soon as you've been here a year. And you know what else? You're in time for our annual picnic! All set? Come in Monday at two for Orientation.

BARBARA. I'm hired? What's the pay?

HOWARD. Depends on the category you're placed in. Nothing left but the drug test! *(He exits.)*

Scene 2

The borrowed apartment. Barbara, Budgie.

Barbara is now in her bathrobe, a gallon water pitcher and glass at her feet.

BARBARA. I said "free apartment!" but there's a catch — I have to baby-sit Budgie, the cockatiel. For the sake of ornithological health and sanity, he has to spend three hours a day out of his cage. Did I mention that birds at close range are one of my very few phobias? *(Budgie squawks and flies off. Barbara pours a glass of water.)* Can't dissolve the trace of weed, but you can flush it — given three days, fifteen gallons of water and a product called Clean P. that sells for 49.95. I read the label: creatinine and uva uris. Bought the ingredients and made my own. Thirty dollars. *(She drinks.)* Somehow, I don't feel triumphant. I'm wondering: How deep is the corrosive effect of humiliation? How many times can you bend before damage sets in? Repetitive stress of the spirit.

Scene 3

Mall-mart, $? per hour. Barbara, Kimberly, Melissa, another associate, Howard.

Barbara enters in blue vest, with name badge, pushing shopping cart full of assorted clothing.

BARBARA. "Orientation" is an eight-hour seminar on:
KIMBERLY and OTHER ASSOCIATE. Mall-mart family values.
BARBARA. Nothing on wages. Last night was a bad one with Budgie. I'm starting my Mall-mart life on four hours sleep. *(She stares around vast space, with no idea what to do or where to go.*

Melissa enters, also in vest and with cart, watches, finally speaks.)

MELISSA. It's confusing, isn't it? Hello. Is this your first day?

BARBARA. You mean it shows? Hi. Ellie sent me to "zone these returns" …

MELISSA. *(Checking first to see no manager is watching.)* You have to learn the labels … *(She expertly separates the piles in Barbara's cart.)* Bobbie Brooks … Kathie Lee … White Stag … Jordache … then the floor. Bobbie's that way today, Kathie's over there, the young lines are in the front. You have to match your models, your colors, your patterns; and keep the size order every time. Then go back to the fitting room for your next load.

BARBARA. Thanks!

MELISSA. Is your name "Barb"?

BARBARA. Actually, it's Barbara.

MELISSA. That's much nicer.

BARBARA. I know. What's yours? I can't read that far.

MELISSA. Melissa. *(They work briskly through the following dialogue. Melissa orders the things customers have scrambled on the rack; Barbara hangs items from the cart; then they team up to empty it, except for misplaced things they've found on the rack.)* What they're featuring today, goes in Image. You gotta keep on top of it: The customers make a beeline. It gets so messed up, right away. Group things by color, and size within each group … Faded Glory? You don't belong in this section. *(Banishes it to the cart, is rewarded with a smile from Barbara.)* … Are you from around here?

BARBARA. I just moved from Florida.

MELISSA. I didn't know people ever left from down there.

BARBARA. I move a lot … Seems true what they say: People are really friendly here.

MELISSA. I never lived anywhere else … Down there, did you work in a store?

BARBARA. First time … 8, 12 … My last job was cleaning houses.

MELISSA. I used to clean too, for a service. Hard work, but I enjoyed the companionship … Here's the one I want, for church. *(Barbara nods appreciation.)* … You have kids?

BARBARA. Boy and girl, grown. You?

MELISSA. Two of each. All of them are in the service. I can't tell you how that sets my mind at rest.

BARBARA. … Athletic Works?

MELISSA. In the cart.

BARBARA. How about you — worked here long?

MELISSA. Six months … Just since I found Jesus … Are you saved?

BARBARA. … Not yet.

MELISSA. He helped me. Put the turquoises next to the greens … Before, I could never be content anyplace. I always blamed the job for my problems. But now that I have a personal relationship with Jesus Christ, I understand that he's testing me. I just wish I'd get Sunday off for worship. Hand me those purples … It's so seldom you get to talk to a person. Liddy was on two weeks before I knew her name. *(They are finished.)* We really made it look nice! Well, nice chatting with you — I better do these returns; you go see what Ellie's got. *(She starts off with cart.)*

BARBARA. Melissa, I need to ask you something.

MELISSA. *(Checks for Howard.)* In a bit. Talking more now is Time Theft.

BARBARA. I need to know how much we make.

MELISSA. Isn't that something, how they don't tell you? Seven dollars an hour. *(On Wage sign, question mark changes to "$7/hr.")* It's okay for me — we own our home, and my husband works construction.

BARBARA. I'm single, and I'm still looking for a place.

MELISSA. Gosh … My niece has been looking for three months! Nobody told you? It's been all over the papers: There's just no place left in this town for working people to live … Oh, my: I'll keep you in my prayers. — Uh, oh, don't look now: Howard's watching!

BARBARA. Howard?

MELISSA. The Assistant Manager! He's coming this way. Go on or he'll write us up! *(Exeunt in opposite directions.)*

Scene 4

Clearview Inn, $245 per week: Barbara, Boyfriend.

Sounds of TV, cars, partying and arguments come through the walls. The room is dimly lit, the parking lot outside is brightly lit: Shadows pass behind the flimsy drawn curtain. Barbara's laptop sits closed on the bed, alongside plastic bags of food, laundry, toiletries, etc. Barbara also sits on bed, in

53

bathrobe, on phone. Boyfriend is on phone elsewhere, his back turned to audience.

BARBARA. You're not getting it. In eight days, I've found *one* listing for "Affordable Studios" … Seven hundred: almost three weeks' pay! The going rate's a thousand a month! … *Yes,* I put my name down, but nothing opens up till next week … Oh, just the worst motel in the country … *Yes,* I have a credit card. *(Boyfriend turns downstage, now we can hear him.)*
BOYFRIEND. Why not use it?
BARBARA. Because I won't.
BOYFRIEND. Why?
BARBARA. Because that's not the point.
BOYFRIEND. Why?
BARBARA. Because other people don't have that option!
BOYFRIEND. You don't want to know what I think, why did you call?
BARBARA. I called for a kind word! *(She hangs up. Boyfriend fades. To audience.)* But hey, no more Budgie. The Clearview Inn. Somebody better update the Internet. Or maybe the false promises are an employer scam, to lure cheap labor to Minneapolis. *(Through what follows, she speaks sometimes to the audience, sometimes to herself. Sorting plastic bags.)* My kitchen … my dining nook. *(Pats the bed.)* Cold plates from the supermarket deli section, hot dishes from the gas station convenience store. Laundry room … medicine cabinet … library, I left home this time … Office! *(Pats closed laptop.)* Why don't I just crank out a chapter? In these surroundings so conducive to contemplation. *(Plucks absently at her robe.)* No air-conditioning, no fan, no window screen. The sheets don't fit the bed. Could write with my finger in the film on that TV screen. The towels! Smell like grease; they have little hairs stuck in them. *(To audience again.)* And the rent for this palace eats my whole *presumptive* check: Mall-mart holds back your first week's pay. They figure with cash in hand, you'd probably head for the border: This way, by the time you get paid, you'll be too worn out and snarled in debt to run. … Find the second job, or pursue the apartment hunt? *(Catches herself plucking.)* Agh! I'm turning into my grandmother! The practical nurse, the model of stoicism who worked into her eighties. She used to do the same thing. Claimed she didn't know she was doing it.

I could get a stronger lightbulb. But that curtain's so flimsy I'd be onstage, displayed to the parking lot. Shut the window and suffocate, or leave it open and invite in all comers?

When did I turn into a wimp?

Scene 5

Emergency Assistance Program: Barbara, social worker.

It's late in the social worker's day.

SOCIAL WORKER. You say you're employed.
BARBARA. Yes.
SOCIAL WORKER. So the problem is...?
BARBARA. Housing. I can't find a place to live.
SOCIAL WORKER. *(Produces a printed card.)* Okay! You need to go to the Housing Crisis Center. *(Barbara is about to protest.)* They'll take your application for housing subsidy, and give you an updated list of affordable apartments. This is the address.
BARBARA. You sent me there this morning. The subsidies are used up for this month. The list's out of date.
SOCIAL WORKER. I saw you this morning?
BARBARA. Uh-huh.
SOCIAL WORKER. ... And you're unemployed.
BARBARA. No, I'm working. At Mall-mart.
SOCIAL WORKER. Oh. You're the third one today ... Okay, I'll tell you the same thing I told the others: Your best bet is to check into a shelter. *(Produces a list.)* Start with St. Theresa's — that's the closest one. *(Checks her watch.)* There should still be beds if you get there in the next hour. They allow ten days, then you can go to the Episcopal Women's Home. That way, you can save up for first and last month's rent.
BARBARA. I was wondering if could get help with food.
SOCIAL WORKER. *(Produces another list.)* Absolutely! Here's a list of the pantries ... But most of them are only open in the morning. For today I'm afraid it's too late.

Scene 6

Mall-mart, $7 per hour. Four customers, Barbara, Kimberly, Melissa, Howard.

Under music, customers cross severally with carts of mainly useless goods: a Fat Lady, pushing a cart piled with clothing; a Timid Man, lost, with clothing and a very large stuffed animal; a Lady in a Sari, with clothing and many boxed electronic items; a Mom with Kids, clothing, economy-size paper goods and a grotesque piece of art or garden statue.

BARBARA. *(Rehangs clothes as she talks to herself.)* Screw you, Howard. "We'll need you to stay an extra hour tonight, but just punch out at your regular time." In other words, we're not going to pay you. *(Mom approaches.)* "Greeting Our Guests" ... "Smile and make eye contact whenever a Guest approaches within ten feet. This is called 'Aggressive Hospitality.'" *(She grins. Mom spots something attractive offstage and exits, ignoring Barbara.)* Pearls before swine. Our Guests are not here for chitchat. They're here to do one thing — shop. *(Timid Man enters, still lost, hesitates, then speaks.)*
TIMID MAN. Excuse me — which way's the cashier?
BARBARA. *(With a big smile.)* Go back to Garden, turn right till you hit the middle aisle, continue past Toys, then the first left. Good luck. *(Timid Man exits doubtfully. Plucking at her clothes as she mutters to herself.)* And why call this the closing shift? The store never closes. The fluorescent lights never go out. "We feed your need, 24/7!" ... In a restaurant, you have actual conversations with different people. When you're a housemaid, you get to snoop in different stuff. At Mall-mart all that changes, day after day, is the layout of the floor. This job could function as an IQ test for the severely cognitively challenged. Autism would be a definite advantage. *(Catches herself plucking.)* Agh! Pretty soon I'll be plucking flesh. Grandma picked big, red holes in herself. *(Fat Lady crosses, heading for the dressing room, holding bra and panties that are plainly too svelte for her. Barbara fixes her with an intentionally incredulous stare; mimes to audience: "Her — in that?" Folds the next item, which is very large.)* Why are so

many Midwesterners *huge?* Deeply embedded cultural preferences. Giant Combo Meals. Super-size Curly Fries — But does anybody think about what that does to me? Forever retrieving, refolding, reshelving, rehanging their fantasies? ... Living with the constant occupational hazard of being crushed in the aisle by some double wide?

HOWARD. *(On mike.)* Attention Mall-mart guests: Please take advantage of our red tag sale. All items with a red tag are twenty percent off! Love Bug bikinis, three for five dollars. Tidy-wee commode covers, 1.99. Inflatable yard pools, now twenty-nine dollars ... *(Customers enter frantically with their carts, tossing items onto Barbara, then exit. Timid man enters, still lost.)*

TIMID MAN. I can't find it.

BARBARA. What?

TIMID MAN. The cashier.

BARBARA. Garden, right to the middle aisle, left after Toys. *(He leaves.)*

BARBARA. ... Why didn't I wait to take dinner — why'd I go at five? Because I needed to sit so bad. ... Why'd I waste my last break at 9:15? Because I hadn't gotten the bad news. 9:15 would have worked if I'd been done at eleven! ... And I threw away four whole minutes, standing in line for a drink! I could've just slurped water from the basin when I stopped to pee! ... Is it worth it to pee again? A forty-second walk, two ways, to steal max, sixty seconds sitting down? *(Catches herself plucking again.)* Stop that! *(She lifts one foot, then the other.)* Midnight ... ! If the bastard had told me sooner, I would have steeled myself and waited till ten ... Would've made it to quarter of, anyway. Oh-h-h. My Reeboks have had the bounce pounded out of them. A whole hour and forty-five minutes to go ... and the foot pain is creeping up my legs. *(Kimberly enters carrying a stack of shirts, watches Barbara work.)*

KIMBERLY. Excuse me: That's a White Stag you're putting in Jordache. *(She continues off.)*

BARBARA. Who's *she?*

HOWARD. *(On mike.)* Attention Mall-mart guests: Please take advantage of our fuschia tag sale. All items with a fuschia tag are thirty percent off. His and Hers Day-glo running suits, 29.99 a pair! M.A.R. 15 assault rifles, $159! *(Customers enter frantically with their carts, tossing items onto Barbara, then exit.)*

BARBARA. *(Correcting the damage.)* Nights and weekends, they come in gangs: Mom, Grandma, and the rugrats, pawing over my clothes, messing up my displays ... Why does Ellie constantly scramble the floor layout? Gotta keep it new for the average customer — who shops Mall-mart three times a week! Why don't these people get a life? *(Customer #1 enters with cart.)* Why should they, when they can motor on over and make mine hell? *(Timid Man enters and approaches her carefully. The face she turns on him makes him flee.)*

HOWARD. *(On mike.)* Attention Mall-mart guests: Please take advantage of our burnt-sienna tag sale! All items with a burnt sienna tag are forty percent off! Turkey-gobbler-themed dish sets, only nineteen dollars! *(Customers enter frantically with their carts, toss items onto Barbara, then exit. Kimberly enters with unicolor stack of T-shirts.)*

KIMBERLY. Are you the one that shelved these items?

BARBARA. ... What?

KIMBERLY. I asked, did you shelve these? Because they're not zoned. Look: Some are ribbed, some are plain. You've got to put 'em in the right place. Did you check the UPC numbers? *(Melissa enters and watches.)*

BARBARA. The UPC numbers? Where do you think we are, the Academy of Sciences? Nobody "checks the UPC numbers"! What do you have, rules for brains? This is the closing shift; I'm not the only one who worked this section today. How many thousand customers came charging through here? It's past ten, I have to stay late, and I have another five loads to go. Do you think possibly, instead of obsessing about T-shirts, you might just help me clean up this floor?

KIMBERLY. *(Nearly in tears.)* Returns aren't my job: My job is to fold and shelve. *(She exits. Melissa sets about picking up the scattered merchandise.)*

BARBARA. Did the thought ever occur to you, that abortion's wasted on the unborn? *(Melissa does not reply. Working.)* "Returns aren't my job." I've never seen the — ! And I didn't hear anybody make her my supervisor. "Some are ribbed, some are plain." Who *is* that Minnie Mouse bitch!? *(The epithet is inspired by Kimberly's hairstyle.)*

MELISSA. That's Kimberly. You don't know her 'cause she only works night relief. She gets home from her day job, then comes in here at nine, after she puts her baby down. *(The wind leaves Barbara's sails. She finds nothing right to say. They pick up all the returns.)*

BARBARA. Thank you.

MELISSA. You still didn't find a place to stay?

BARBARA. Not yet.

MELISSA. I brought you something — I hope you don't mind. *(Hands her a brown bag.)* In case you still didn't have a kitchen. I made you a chicken salad sandwich.
BARBARA. Thank you.
MELISSA. Are you mad?
BARBARA. Not at you. *(Howard enters.)*
HOWARD. You two: Go and punch out, then come back and finish these returns. *(They exit.)* Now you're thinking, "How can he do that? How can he make them work without pay?" It's not me. And it's not my manager. It's not even his manager — it's the numbers … The numbers make the decisions. Takes the personal element out of it. That's what's great about how corporations work.

We don't have quotas, but we do have targets. For the company, each division, each store, each department within each store. And if our store's not hitting its target, there's two things we can do. We can increase sales, which we work very hard at with specials and promotions. And we can cut costs. Now our building costs and shipping costs are fixed. Price of inventory, we don't control. Only one cost is flexible: labor.

Now, when I ask my Associates for a little bit more, it's way, way less than I give. I work sixty or seventy hours, and my paycheck says I worked forty. An Associate doesn't show up, the Department Manager covers their job. Who covers her job, along with his own? Where the buck stops: the Assistant Manager. But my work pays off, in my profit share. Associates could get a share, too, if they stayed. But out of fifty-six I had last year, I had to replace forty-four. Because these people steal. They take drugs. They file false claims for workman's comp. Mainly, they just disappear.

I believe in the market. The market pays everyone exactly what they're worth. I'm gonna prove it. I saw you at Intermission: pretty upscale crowd — I'm guessing not many of you shop at Mall-mart. Some of you probably support "living wage" laws. Okay — are you ready to wash your own car? Pay a third more on your restaurant bill? Pay hardware store prices at Home Depot? No way, right? See how it works? It's not you, it's not me. The numbers decide. *(He exits.)*

Scene 7

A phone booth: Barbara, (elsewhere) Boyfriend.

Barbara enters with a cardboard box full of food.

BARBARA. *(To audience.)* One thing really great about working the closing shift: You can make it to the food pantries! Honey Nut Chex ... Sugar cookies ... Barbecue sauce ... Tootsie Rolls ... Kool Aid ... ooh, peanut butter! ... A canned ham! Ooh, I'm gonna splurge: Buy a stick of butter and a sweet potato. Because tomorrow, I'll have a stove and refrigerator!

Hello, Hopkins Park Plaza? ... This is Barbara, the one who's moving in today. I need to know when you're gonna be in? ... I came by — 5-G ... *What?* It was supposed to be vacant day before yesterday! ... Another week!? ... You can't do this. I moved out of my motel because you said I could move in! ... Okay, not you. The man said. Louis said. Maybe *he* wants to pay my hotel bill! I had to stay at the Comfort Inn, and it costs more than I make! ... *"Doesn't work there anymore"?* ... That doesn't let you off the hook. You owe me, you have to give me something! ... "Without a kitchen"? ... It has to be okay. When? ... Next *week?* ... "Call Monday." That's five days from now. I'm living on my credit card. Five days is not — five days won't — *(She hears a click.)* Hello? ... Hello? *(She hangs up. She is at a loss. After a moment, she dials a number, calling home. Elsewhere, Boyfriend enters but can't get ringing cell phone out of his pocket. Barbara changes her mind just as he succeeds, and hangs up.)*
BOYFRIEND. Hello? *(No one is there. He checks display and calls back. Barbara listens to the phone ring till he hangs up and exits.)*

Scene 8

Mall-mart, $7 per hour. Barbara, Melissa, Howard.

Barbara and Melissa enter pushing carts.

BARBARA. What do I do? All my stuff's in my car. I want to know what people do! Melissa, I'm on the street!

MELISSA. Now listen. I've thought about it. I want you to come stay with me.

BARBARA. Oh, I couldn't ...

MELISSA. Just till your place comes vacant. This way, you can save for your deposit.

BARBARA. I still couldn't save enough.

MELISSA. You could if you were making nine dollars an hour.

BARBARA. How?

MELISSA. My sister-in-law got on at Twin Cities Plastics — they're hiring! They pay nine dollars, and benefits! Health insurance! And that got me thinking. Seven dollars is just not enough for what they put us through. We both ought to apply at Twin Cities. I'm going Monday and take the test, want to come?

BARBARA. I've been wanting to try factory work ...

MELISSA. I want you to move in tonight.

BARBARA. ... What does your husband say?

MELISSA. Arnold? He says it's okay.

BARBARA. If it's not a huge problem ... I don't even have to pack ... You really think you can stand me for a week?

MELISSA. *(Works.)* One thing, I don't want you to be scared of our dogs. They're attack dogs: You need them in our neighborhood, but Arnold has them very well trained ... *(Barbara returns to work.)* Now, he's taken the girls' room for his guns and things so I can't offer you privacy, but we have a sofabed in the dining room that everyone says is really comfortable ... And — *(Working harder.)* — well, sometimes you might hear Arnold say ugly things to me, but that's not really him: He knows better, he's trying to be better. I told him, "We have a good bed going to waste, and I have a friend who doesn't even have a roof!" That's not all I told him. I said, "This is not just your house: It's my house, too." No telling what I might say to him if I start making nine dollars.

BARBARA. Melissa … I can't.

MELISSA. Can't what?

BARBARA. I actually have a job.

MELISSA. I didn't know you were looking.

BARBARA. Not that kind of job. I'm a writer.

MELISSA. Oh.

BARBARA. I'm writing a book about work — this place'll be one of the chapters. I'm going to write about all the rules, about Howard, about you, saving my life. *(Melissa is silent.)* See, the point was to see if I could make it without help, so actually, if I stayed with someone …

MELISSA. A writer. Well, you probably have a place to stay.

BARBARA. Not here. In Minneapolis, no. I'll never forget that you offered. I would never have made it this long, without you … I guess I'm leaving town. I guess today's my last day. Will you give me your address? *(Finds a piece of paper in her pocket. Melissa looks around for Howard, then writes on the torn paper.)*

MELISSA. Maybe you can send me a postcard of a palm tree.

BARBARA. Actually, I'm not going back to Florida. I think I'm going to move near my daughter, in Virginia.

MELISSA. Well. I'm definitely going to try at Twin Cities. I don't know if I could even stand to keep on here without someone else who likes to talk. *(Howard enters.)* Don't look, just go. *(Exits, trailed by Howard. Barbara watches her all the way off.)*

BARBARA. … By this hour, there's no world beyond the store doors. No night sky, just fluorescent lights. But in an hour and a half, I'm going out there. Back to the other world of e-mail and appointments, where Barbara lives, and enjoys the luxury of understanding. She doesn't hate the customers. She's not scared of Howard. She wouldn't take her rage out on Kimberly. That's Barb. Her father never clambered out of the mines. She wouldn't turn down Melissa's spare bed. She works at Mall-mart for real. *(She exits.)*

EPILOGUE

Gail, Pete, Hector, Joan, Melissa, Holly, Maddy, Marge, George, Barbara, Carlie.

GAIL. I met someone. Night my car died. I'm standin' on the street with the hood up, blubbering. I hear this voice. "Bet it's your alternator." Deep, like the low string on a bass fiddle: I was always a sucker for that sound. And that lost cowboy look. Cyril. Rides rodeo, and off-season he's a roofer. Trailer's small for two, but that don't matter when you're in love.

PETE. Surprise: I'm still here. Thought you'd like to know, the one who threw milk on Barbara kicked the bucket.

HECTOR. Philip, one day he catch me — *(Mimes drinking.)* Fire my ass. I go get a six-pack. Go to my kids' school, tell the principal, "Is an emergency": I take us all to the beach. Next morning, get the paper, need a fry cook at Chevy's. *Cabron* do me a favor. I make a dollar an hour more.

JOAN. You are gonna love this. Philip got fired for stealing!

MELISSA. I got on at the plastics factory. Nine dollars makes a big difference. And I have every Sunday off, which is a balm to my spirit!

JOAN. This was after he fired Hector for drinking, and hired an idiot who can't read orders and don't know a Snuffy from a Daisy Mae. We got a new manager, Norman, he made us all do the pee-pee test. And Days' Inn got a new manager too, so I gotta find a new parking spot.

PETE. Linda left. The owners want to sell to a chain. I plan on going into real estate. Either that or have a website, start a business on line. Soon as I get a computer.

MELISSA. One thing about the factory, sometimes the air makes me sick. I told my supervisor and she said, "You can work through it." I've asked Jesus and he'll tell me what I should do.

MADDY. This writer asked me once, was I jealous of rich people, all they have? I said, "Hell, no, who'd want to have so much stuff you have to hire somebody to clean it?" I lied. There is one thing I'm jealous of. They get to take a vacation.

HOLLY. When Ted gives me a raise, that's his way of saying, "Holly, I appreciate your good work — thank you, Holly." And that challenges me to always go the extra mile, and find ways to do even better. I'm the only girl that ever got maternity leave: two weeks, at full pay! I've gotten three raises just since I got to be Team Leader: I'm at 7.80 an hour. Maddy's still carrying on like always, so she's still at 6.65.

MARGE. Last week we were working in a house? And Holly made me do kitchen, but it turned out I was lucky, because I had to work around the lady and she was gonna have a party, and she was making her own canapés. She had these tiny, tiny toast slices that either had a clam on 'em and a hot, hot pepper, or a dot a' baked ricotta cheese and two colors of sliced olives. Anyway, she offered me to sample 'em. Well, they looked so delicious I said, "I'm not supposed to, but if you won't tell … " and she promised she wouldn't, and I did not care. I ate two of each.

GEORGE. Hello! How ya'all doin'!? I am speaking good English now. I have good job. I am manager at McDonald's. Now *I* watch nobody don't steal from dry storage! *(To someone offstage.)* Hey! Buddy! What you do — what are you doing? *(Barbara has finished a lecture, and is taking questions from the audience.)*

BARBARA. … Below the poverty line? Of fifteen thousand a year for a mom and two kids? Thirty-two million people. You know how the government draws that line? Minimum food budget, times three. Three times *rent* and you'd still be poor at *thirty* thousand. This way, they wipe out so much poverty! *(A second question.)* Well … We do it for the *middle* class: I get *my* housing subsidized, twenty thousand dollars a year … Mortgage interest deduction. *(A third questioner asks: "Can you sum up your book?")* Our whole lives are subsidized. By the working poor. They're our biggest anonymous donors.

CARLIE. When the Comfort Inn done laid me off, thought I 'uz gon' be on the street with a cup. People say, "When you in trouble, go to some church, tell the people there what you need." So I went down to Macedonian Baptist. Stand outside on a Sunday with a sign I made: "Will clean or take care of seniors for room and board." And sure enough, a lady come up to me and say she need help with her mother. I cook, clean, get the ol' lady dressed, get her up, get her down, take her to the bathroom … nights, I got to put her on a diaper. She a big woman, too. But she a smoker, and she got her pension. Always got cigarettes. I don' need to steal 'em, she offer 'em. I got my own room, with a TV. I got it made, for now.

End of Play

64

PROPERTY LIST

Slide projector and slides
Microphone
Laden waitress tray
Bus tray
Phone
Cigarette and lighter/matches
Money
Clothes
Dishes (clean and dirty)
Cleaning rags
Cleaning products
Shopping cart
Clothes hangers
Coffeepot (BARBARA)
Pitcher of water (BARBARA)
Condiment caddy (NITA)
Order book (NITA, BARBARA)
Menus (BARBARA)
Pen/pencil (BARBARA, EDITOR)
Bill (GAIL, SERVER
Bus stand (GAIL)
Tablecloth (SERVER)
Wine (SERVER)
Food (SERVER, HECTOR)
Credit card (EDITOR)
Computer (BARBARA)
Computer printout (MANAGER, HOWARD)
Paper cup (MANAGER)
Purse (BARBARA)
Want ads (BARBARA)
Ashtray (BARBARA)
Ibuprofen (JOAN)
Soup pot (BARBARA)
Sauce pan (BARBARA)
Two cans of soup (BARBARA)
Wooden spoon (BARBARA)
Bag of lentils (BARBARA)
Jar of bay leaves (BARBARA)
Silverware (GAIL, BARBARA)

Napkins (GAIL, BARBARA)
Cleaning cart (CARLIE, BARBARA, HOLLY)
Towels (CARLIE)
Package of hot dog rolls (BARBARA)
Sandwich (CARLIE)
Condom (BARBARA)
Remote control (CARLIE)
Take-out orders (JOAN)
Mushrooms (GAIL)
Knife (GAIL, BARBARA)
Half-pint bottle of vodka (HECTOR)
Bell (HECTOR)
Tomatoes (GAIL)
Drinking glasses (GEORGE, BARBARA)
Serving utensil (HECTOR)
Salad (BARBARA)
Keys (BARBARA)
Rolling suitcase (BARBARA)
Vacuum cleaner (HOLLY, MADDY)
Brita water pitcher (STAGE MANAGER)
Water bottle (BARBARA)
Glass of iced tea (RICH LADY)
Protein bar (BARBARA)
Four breakfast trays (BARBARA)
Bag of frozen peas (MADDY)
Plastic bags (BARBARA)
Printed card (SOCIAL WORKER)
Lists (SOCIAL WORKER)
Stuffed animal (TIMID MAN)
Boxed electronic items (LADY IN SARI)
Economy-size paper goods (MOM WITH KID)
Grotesque piece of art or garden statue (MOM WITH KIDS)
Various "Mall-Mart" items (CUSTOMERS)
Brown-bag lunch (MELISSA)
Cardboard box full of food (BARBARA)
Cell phone (BOYFRIEND)
Piece of paper (BARBARA)

SOUND EFFECTS

Kitchen bell
Music
Dishes crashing
Dishwasher yelling
Voiceover
Scream
Sound of person and vacuum cleaner falling and landing
Sounds of TV, cars, partying, arguments
Ringing cell phone
Pay phone ringing

NEW PLAYS

★ **THE EXONERATED by Jessica Blank and Erik Jensen.** Six interwoven stories paint a picture of an American criminal justice system gone horribly wrong and six brave souls who persevered to survive it. "The #1 play of the year...intense and deeply affecting..." *–NY Times.* "Riveting. Simple, honest storytelling that demands reflection." *–A.P.* "Artful and moving...pays tribute to the resilience of human hearts and minds." *–Variety.* "Stark...riveting...cunningly orchestrated." *–The New Yorker.* "Hard-hitting, powerful, and socially relevant." *–Hollywood Reporter.* [7M, 3W] ISBN: 0-8222-1946-8

★ **STRING FEVER by Jacquelyn Reingold.** Lily juggles the big issues: turning forty, artificial insemination and the elusive scientific Theory of Everything in this Off-Broadway comedy hit. "Applies the elusive rules of string theory to the conundrums of one woman's love life. Think *Sex and the City* meets *Copenhagen.*" *–NY Times.* "A funny offbeat and touching look at relationships...an appealing romantic comedy populated by oddball characters." *–NY Daily News.* "Where kooky, zany, and madcap meet...whimsically winsome." *–NY Magazine.* "STRING FEVER will have audience members happily stringing along." *–TheaterMania.com.* "Reingold's language is surprising, inventive, and unique." *–nytheatre.com.* "...[a] whimsical comic voice." *–Time Out.* [3M, 3W (doubling)] ISBN: 0-8222-1952-2

★ **DEBBIE DOES DALLAS adapted by Erica Schmidt, composed by Andrew Sherman, conceived by Susan L. Schwartz.** A modern morality tale told as a comic musical of tragic proportions as the classic film is brought to the stage. "A scream! A saucy, tongue-in-cheek romp." *–The New Yorker.* "Hilarious! DEBBIE manages to have it all: beauty, brains and a great sense of humor!" *–Time Out.* "Shamelessly silly, shrewdly self-aware and proud of being naughty. Great fun!" *–NY Times.* "Racy and raucous, a lighthearted, fast-paced thoroughly engaging and hilarious send-up." *–NY Daily News.* [3M, 5W] ISBN: 0-8222-1955-7

★ **THE MYSTERY PLAYS by Roberto Aguirre-Sacasa.** Two interrelated one acts, loosely based on the tradition of the medieval mystery plays. "... stylish, spine-tingling...Mr. Aguirre-Sacasa uses standard tricks of horror stories, borrowing liberally from masters like Kafka, Lovecraft, Hitchcock...But his mastery of the genre is his own...irresistible." *–NY Times.* "Undaunted by the special-effects limitations of theatre, playwright and *Marvel* comicbook writer Roberto Aguirre-Sacasa maps out some creepy twilight zones in THE MYSTERY PLAYS, an engaging, related pair of one acts...The theatre may rarely deliver shocks equivalent to, say, *Dawn of the Dead*, but Aguirre-Sacasa's work is fine compensation." *–Time Out.* [4M, 2W] ISBN: 0-8222-2038-5

★ **THE JOURNALS OF MIHAIL SEBASTIAN by David Auburn.** This epic one-man play spans eight tumultuous years and opens a uniquely personal window on the Romanian Holocaust and the Second World War. "Powerful." *–NY Times.* "[THE JOURNALS OF MIHAIL SEBASTIAN] allows us to glimpse the idiosyncratic effects of that awful history on one intelligent, pragmatic, recognizably real man..." *–NY Newsday.* [3M, 5W] ISBN: 0-8222-2006-7

★ **LIVING OUT by Lisa Loomer.** The story of the complicated relationship between a Salvadoran nanny and the Anglo lawyer she works for. "A stellar new play. Searingly funny." *–The New Yorker.* "Both generous and merciless, equally enjoyable and disturbing." *–NY Newsday.* "A bitingly funny new comedy. The plight of working mothers is explored from two pointedly contrasting perspectives in this sympathetic, sensitive new play." *–Variety.* [2M, 6W] ISBN: 0-8222-1994-8

DRAMATISTS PLAY SERVICE, INC.
440 Park Avenue South, New York, NY 10016 212-683-8960 Fax 212-213-1539
postmaster@dramatists.com   www.dramatists.com

NEW PLAYS

★ **MATCH by Stephen Belber.** Mike and Lisa Davis interview a dancer and choreographer about his life, but it is soon evident that their agenda will either ruin or inspire them—and definitely change their lives forever. "Prolific laughs and ear-to-ear smiles." *–NY Magazine.* "Uproariously funny, deeply moving, enthralling theater. Stephen Belber's MATCH has great beauty and tenderness, and abounds in wit." *–NY Daily News.* "Three and a half out of four stars." *–USA Today.* "A theatrical steeplechase that leads straight from outrageous bitchery to unadorned, heartfelt emotion." *–Wall Street Journal.* [2M, 1W] ISBN: 0-8222-2020-2

★ **HANK WILLIAMS: LOST HIGHWAY by Randal Myler and Mark Harelik.** The story of the beloved and volatile country-music legend Hank Williams, featuring twenty-five of his most unforgettable songs. "[LOST HIGHWAY has] the exhilarating feeling of Williams on stage in a particular place on a particular night...serves up classic country with the edges raw and the energy hot...By the end of the play, you've traveled on a profound emotional journey: LOST HIGHWAY transports its audience and communicates the inspiring message of the beauty and richness of Williams' songs...forceful, clear-eyed, moving, impressive." *–Rolling Stone.* "...honors a very particular musical talent with care and energy... smart, sweet, poignant." *–NY Times.* [7M, 3W] ISBN: 0-8222-1985-9

★ **THE STORY by Tracey Scott Wilson.** An ambitious black newspaper reporter goes against her editor to investigate a murder and finds the *best* story...but at what cost? "A singular new voice...deeply emotional, deeply intellectual, and deeply musical..." *–The New Yorker.* "...a conscientious and absorbing new drama..." *–NY Times.* "...a riveting, tough-minded drama about race, reporting and the truth..." *–A.P.* "... a stylish, attention-holding script that ends on a chilling note that will leave viewers with much to talk about." *–Curtain Up.* [2M, 7W (doubling, flexible casting)] ISBN: 0-8222-1998-0

★ **OUR LADY OF 121st STREET by Stephen Adly Guirgis.** The body of Sister Rose, beloved Harlem nun, has been stolen, reuniting a group of life-challenged childhood friends who square off as they wait for her return. "A scorching and dark new comedy... Mr. Guirgis has one of the finest imaginations for dialogue to come along in years." *–NY Times.* "Stephen Guirgis may be the best playwright in America under forty." *–NY Magazine.* [8M, 4W] ISBN: 0-8222-1965-4

★ **HOLLYWOOD ARMS by Carrie Hamilton and Carol Burnett.** The coming-of-age story of a dreamer who manages to escape her bleak life and follow her romantic ambitions to stardom. Based on Carol Burnett's bestselling autobiography, *One More Time.* "...pure theatre and pure entertainment..." *–Talkin' Broadway.* "...a warm, fuzzy evening of theatre." *–BrodwayBeat.com.* "...chuckles and smiles of recognition or surprise flow naturally...a remarkable slice of life." *–TheatreScene.net.* [5M, 5W, 1 girl] ISBN: 0-8222-1959-X

★ **INVENTING VAN GOGH by Steven Dietz.** A haunting and hallucinatory drama about the making of art, the obsession to create and the fine line that separates truth from myth. "Like a van Gogh painting, Dietz's story is a gorgeous example of excess—one that remakes reality with broad, well-chosen brush strokes. At evening's end, we're left with the author's resounding opinions on art and artifice, and provoked by his constant query into which is greater: van Gogh's art or his violent myth." *–Phoenix New Times.* "Dietz's writing is never simple. It is always brilliant. Shaded, compressed, direct, lucid—he frames his subject with a remarkable understanding of painting as a physical experience." *–Tucson Citizen.* [4M, 1W] ISBN: 0-8222-1954-9

DRAMATISTS PLAY SERVICE, INC.
440 Park Avenue South, New York, NY 10016 212-683-8960 Fax 212-213-1539
postmaster@dramatists.com   www.dramatists.com

NEW PLAYS

★ **INTIMATE APPAREL by Lynn Nottage.** The moving and lyrical story of a turn-of-the-century black seamstress whose gifted hands and sewing machine are the tools she uses to fashion her dreams from the whole cloth of her life's experiences. "…Nottage's play has a delicacy and eloquence that seem absolutely right for the time she is depicting…" *–NY Daily News.* "…thoughtful, affecting…The play offers poignant commentary on an era when the cut and color of one's dress—and of course, skin—determined whom one could and could not marry, sleep with, even talk to in public." *–Variety.* [2M, 4W] ISBN: 0-8222-2009-1

★ **BROOKLYN BOY by Donald Margulies.** A witty and insightful look at what happens to a writer when his novel hits the bestseller list. "The characters are beautifully drawn, the dialogue sparkles…" *–nytheatre.com.* "Few playwrights have the mastery to smartly investigate so much through a laugh-out-loud comedy that combines the vintage subject matter of successful writer-returning-to-ethnic-roots with the familiar mid-life crisis." *–Show Business Weekly.* [4M, 3W] ISBN: 0-8222-2074-1

★ **CROWNS by Regina Taylor.** Hats become a springboard for an exploration of black history and identity in this celebratory musical play. "Taylor pulls off a Hat Trick: She scores thrice, turning CROWNS into an artful amalgamation of oral history, fashion show, and musical theater…" *–TheatreMania.com.* "…wholly theatrical…Ms. Taylor has created a show that seems to arise out of spontaneous combustion, as if a bevy of department-store customers simultaneously decided to stage a revival meeting in the changing room." *–NY Times.* [1M, 6W (2 musicians)] ISBN: 0-8222-1963-8

★ **EXITS AND ENTRANCES by Athol Fugard.** The story of a relationship between a young playwright on the threshold of his career and an aging actor who has reached the end of his. "[Fugard] can say more with a single line than most playwrights convey in an entire script…Paraphrasing the title, it's safe to say this drama, making its memorable entrance into our consciousness, is unlikely to exit as long as a theater exists for exceptional work." *–Variety.* "A thought-provoking, elegant and engrossing new play…" *–Hollywood Reporter.* [2M] ISBN: 0-8222-2041-5

★ **BUG by Tracy Letts.** A thriller featuring a pair of star-crossed lovers in an Oklahoma City motel facing a bug invasion, paranoia, conspiracy theories and twisted psychological motives. "…obscenely exciting…top-flight craftsmanship. Buckle up and brace yourself…" *–NY Times.* "…[a] thoroughly outrageous and thoroughly entertaining play…the possibility of enemies, real and imagined, to squash has never been more theatrical." *–A.P.* [3M, 2W] ISBN: 0-8222-2016-4

★ **THOM PAIN (BASED ON NOTHING) by Will Eno.** An ordinary man muses on childhood, yearning, disappointment and loss, as he draws the audience into his last-ditch plea for empathy and enlightenment. "It's one of those treasured nights in the theater—treasured nights anywhere, for that matter—that can leave you both breathless with exhilaration and…in a puddle of tears." *–NY Times.* "Eno's words…are familiar, but proffered in a way that is constantly contradictory to our expectations. Beckett is certainly among his literary ancestors." *–nytheatre.com.* [1M] ISBN: 0-8222-2076-8

★ **THE LONG CHRISTMAS RIDE HOME by Paula Vogel.** Past, present and future collide on a snowy Christmas Eve for a troubled family of five. "…[a] lovely and hauntingly original family drama…a work that breathes so much life into the theater." *–Time Out.* "…[a] delicate visual feast…" *–NY Times.* "…brutal and lovely…the overall effect is magical." *–NY Newsday.* [3M, 3W] ISBN: 0-8222-2003-2

DRAMATISTS PLAY SERVICE, INC.
440 Park Avenue South, New York, NY 10016 212-683-8960 Fax 212-213-1539
postmaster@dramatists.com www.dramatists.com